To Bob...
  who through SPRC
helped me write this
book

                Tom

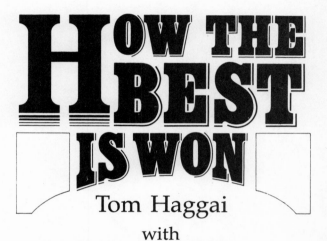

HOW THE BEST IS WON

Tom Haggai

with
Richard L. Federer

THOMAS NELSON PUBLISHERS
Nashville • Camden • Kansas City

To Buren
. . . the constancy of my life

Published in Nashville, Tennessee, by Thomas Nelson, Inc., and dis-
tributed in Canada by Lawson Falle, Ltd., Cambridge, Ontario.

Printed in the United States of America.

Scripture quotations are from THE NEW KING JAMES VERSION of the Bible.
Copyright © 1979, 1980, 1982, Thomas Nelson, Inc., Publishers.

J. B. Phillips: THE NEW TESTAMENT IN MODERN ENGLISH, Revised
Edition. © J. B. Phillips 1958, 1960, 1972. Used by permission of Mac-
millan Publishing Co., Inc.

CONTENTS

teams ferret out facts, while consultants wrestle with "what if's," the leader initiates innovation.

Foreword

It is difficult to imagine a more demanding audience for a
public speaker to face than the college convocation, a
collection of critical minds assembled, fairly certain that
most of what the speaker would say, they already know. It
is a formidable challenge. Yet, year after year, Tom Haggai
has not only met this challenge at Pepperdine University,
but he has made many converts to his unique mode of
thinking.

Tom searches behind the logic and hard realities of life to
find the motivational engines that drive them. He looks
under the hood of America's leading corporations and
businesses to show us the attitudes of their leaders, most of
whom he knows in a warm and personal way.

Although Tom travels thousands of miles and addresses
hundreds of groups each year, I have long wished that he
would "bottle" this wisdom writ upon wind and transcribe
it on paper for a wider audience. As this volume carries you
back to the frontiers of the Old West, and forward to the
new frontiers of the twenty-first century, I think you will
find Tom Haggai's unique pattern of thinking both
compelling and contagious.

Dr. David Davenport
President
Pepperdine University

Preface

We've all gone West.

Have you chased the rustlers with Tom Mix? ridden the range with Hopalong Cassidy? stood against the odds with only Tonto at your side as the Lone Ranger? trailed tough hombres, bringing a little civility to the hunt by singing along with Gene Autry? swooped down upon your ranch with Sky King? joined Hoss and the boys with father Ben Cartwright?

How did you go West? By riding a broomstick around the backyard? Or by transforming a sawhorse into "Hi Ho Silver," claiming the family's three-generation rocking horse?

Do you still have that picture taken on your sixth birthday of you dressed in chaps, ornamental vest, six-gun strapped on your right leg, lasso hooked to your belt, red bandana around your neck, and cowboy hat perched over your left eye?

In later years did you feel like Roy Rogers and one of the Sons of the Pioneers when you sat around a community bonfire and sang about tumbleweeds? Or did you express your independence by belting out "Don't Fence Me In"?

The West is an integral part of each of us. Inculcated in our minds is the obligation to reach out beyond ourselves to make things bigger and better. Horace Greeley's advice to "Go West, young man," was a call for enlightened dissatisfaction with what we had compared to what we could carve out. When a youthful president wanted to shake our nation from its lethargy, he pushed us to a New Frontier. John Kennedy now wanted us "to make the world safe for diversity" as we had the West.

With alarm I have witnessed our nation moving from a spirit of pioneering to a spirit of surviving. *Status quo* was once considered a subversive term. Not today. We are now reacting, not acting. Strength is now measured by one's having the stability to do the same thing in the same way for the same people. We compliment ourselves: "We're just doin' what *brung* us here."

The West symbolized a fluid society. Trying to see beyond the horizon kept our thinking stimulated, prevented our systems from becoming sacrosanct, moved obsolete manufacturing plants from being shrines, and cautioned our staffs against counting how many they were instead of how much work they accomplished. Irony! As the world has developed a single marketplace with the farthest frontier only a *Concorde* away, we have become inflexible rather than adaptable. We've become rigid, not responsive. The broader the frontier, the more nearsighted we've become. Our transaction ability is too much for our traditional markets. We have a global frontier unsettled economically, socially, and politically, but we're reluctant to move out.

While best sellers abound with succinct, simple, smooth rules for instant success, I have chosen to share observations from four decades of thinking and speaking, reaching back to the time of my first corporate address. I call you to once again cross the Mississippi and move into the unknown, trusting not "six coined cliches" but a thinking pattern that admits fear having a greater faith—one that experiences self-doubt but responds with self-discipline; one that accepts failure but turns retreat to resolution. This book is written for the quiet times to set a mood, to catch a spirit, of wanting not only to do things better but to do better things.

Yes, I am convinced the steepest and most neglected slope of the learning curve is attitude, not aptitude. Atmosphere is more important than skills. Our capacity to habitate new frontiers depends on our applied imagination more than our acquired knowledge. Broad understanding is valued more than specialized talent.

Yes, I have anthropomorphized the corporation believing that no matter how large the company, it is still the extension and reflection of its leadership. Through the years the corporate stocks that my wife, Buren, and I have bought for estate building were purchased not on the basis of an analyst's advice but on the simple fact of who leads the corporation. With the heart of a romanticist, I've dressed the leaders described in this book in Western garb and placed them on today's frontiers. I want to show the heart behind the head. We've become familiar with the leaders' *methods and mechanics* but I want to show the warmth of their *missions and motivations*. There is, however, no attempt to make "plaster saints" out of any I mention, nor any reason to highlight the obvious—that we all have feet of clay. There is a disproportionate number of executives related to the food industry simply because it's the business I see most and know best.

No room has been set aside for the business narcissists, our newest entrepreneurial pretenders. Their biographies, hyped by top-paid publicists, would be comic relief if they didn't take themselves so seriously, thus becoming dangerous to us all. They pose as "corporate populists" protecting the worth of the shareholders from the mismanagement of the "good ol' boys" who are the CEO's of too many of our corporations. The points of attack are on the amount of stock the CEO owns and the perks including the clubs and resorts where he is membered. They know the clubs so well, you sense they are motivated by rejection. The contemporary breed of corporate wreckers do not create jobs or lasting wealth. In fact, they are the beneficiaries of the very corporations they disrupt. It has always been my feeling that if you choose to bite the hand that feeds you, you should at least take out your teeth and "gum it to death."

I wonder why I would be brazen enough to write this book. My fascination with leadership and my desire to be part of the twenty-first century wagon train, I inherited from a lady who never viewed herself as a leader. Her maternal roots were planted in Maine during the latter 1600s, and her father came from Nova Scotia. As powerful as she was gentle, Mildred Steere Haggai was my mother. It would have been easier for her to die than to live at my birth. Yet, she believed God made us to live. Being the youngest by several years, I received the attention an only child might experience. Besides sharing my grandfather's interest in my baseball playing, she literally stuffed me full of biographies. As I met these leaders through the printed page, she made me aware that I must assume *personal* responsibility for the *general* welfare of the world about me. She never allowed me to think I had greater ability than I possessed but also never let me use my limitations as an excuse for lack of effort. She made me understand that honors were only deserved if they aided me in being more honorable. For the forty-seven years I knew her, she drew very few painless breaths; yet, she believed she could face any need in the neighborhood and do something to help.

Mildred Steere Haggai gave me the courage to face every challenge—nervous, maybe,—believing one person *can* and *must* make a difference. She raised me believing the words of Boston clergyman and author, Edward Everett Hale:

I am only one, but I am one.
I cannot do everything, but I can do something.
I will not let that which I cannot do
Keep me from doing what I can do.

That may be the way for the best to be won.

1

The Cavalry Ain't Comin'

"**O**ne of them always comes back," whispered the grizzled old cowboy, rubbing his backside against the crumbling earth of the shallow arroyo.

"Keep your head down. It might be another redskin trick," grunted his youthful companion. "Can you make out whose horse it is?"

"Naw," spat the oldtimer, "but soon as the sun clears the canyon wall . . ."

"They'll attack again," shivered the boy. "This time we're done for. They've killed everybody but us!"

"Not quite," muttered the wagon master, lifting his white-bearded chin above the edge of the gully. Through the predawn gloom, he slowly surveyed the scene: broken and burned-out wagons, dead men and horses, overturned and scattered boxes of supplies. His wagon train West was dead in its tracks.

From somewhere behind the pile of broken dreams, he could hear a soft whimper, like that of a woman all spent from crying.

"I can hear Miss Ellie, still."

As the sun slowly rose in the east, a cloud of red dust obscured it. The Indians were attacking again.

▌▐▌

From my vantage point in the front row of the Center Theatre in Brockton, Massachusetts, I could count all those Indians . . . at least eighteen "skillion" dozen of them.

Nervously, I grabbed handfuls of popcorn and threw them

15

at my gaping mouth, missing half the time to the delight of the kid behind me who couldn't afford any. "How in the world," I wondered, "did we Americans ever get to California or Oregon with the Indians killing all of our pioneers there on the plains of Nebraska?"

Grabbing my Orange Crush for one last belt, I was ready to jump from my seat, crawl into that gully, and be a hero.

Then I heard it . . . just barely. Or was it my hope playing tricks on me? I heard it . . . yes, I did, louder and louder. I heard the bugle (back then we didn't know it was just Kemper Insurance on the way to settle a claim). There they were: two dozen cavalrymen forming two blue lines, flags flying, horses charging, and being led by their sergeant major, none other than the big Duke himself—John Wayne. They had ridden all night but didn't have one speck of dust on their gleaming black boots. Each trooper's white hat was centered on his head, unjostled by the hard ride.

John Wayne led because he was the only fellow on the movie lot who could hold the pennant with his left hand while accurately aiming with his right arm. (Somewhere I read, "After all, you can't lead a cavalry charge if you look funny riding a horse.")

It was all sound and fury, measured gunshots and whizzing arrows, but I knew how it would end and I felt good. Soon the Indians tucked tail and headed for the hills.

I remember taking my empty popcorn bag, blowing it up and slamming it with my fist, joining the rest of the kids in cannons of celebration. We created a second explosion by stomping our empty cups on the floor. I mean, this was the good old U.S. of A! This was what America was all about. Anytime you had a problem, anytime you ever thought about surrender, anytime you were ready to throw in the towel, anytime there seemed to be no light in the darkness, all you had to do was "suck it up"—take the deep breath, hang in there a second longer—because the cavalry was always on the way to save you.

I, and many others in business leadership positions today were just kids when we saw that Saturday matinee movie, but we haven't gotten over it yet. We still believe deep in our hearts that no matter what the trouble, somebody, somewhere is on the way to our rescue. But when we're snapped out of our memories, the naked truth confronts us: The cavalry ain't comin'.

Today's Reality: No Quick Fix

Today's leader stands conspicuously alone and vulnerable.

Whatever difficulties and dangers are imposed on us—whether corporate, political, family, or personal—we're going to have to solve them on our own. No cunningly designed program, no sleight-of-hand accounting, no "quick fix" is coming to save us.

Today's generation of leaders can't recall the pseudo-superiority resulting from our victories in World War II. We don't have instant ingredients that need only a pot, water, heat, and a few seconds to cook. As H. L. Mencken wrote, "There's always an easy solution to every problem . . . neat, plausible . . . and *wrong!*"

Enlightened leadership today speaks of solving problems as only one alternative. They understand that removing mountains is seldom feasible, so they must decide whether to tunnel through, go around, or climb over.

On March 15, 1986, IBM's Thomas J. Watson, Jr., addressing the national meeting of Physicians for Social Responsibility corroborated this complexity by declaring, "I am a businessman, and I have learned to deal with things as they are and not as I would like them to be." And Harry B. Schacht of Cummins Engines says, "Operate in the world the way it is, not the way you wish it were."

We were served well by 1985. Filled with memories, we marked the fortieth anniversary of VJ Day and realized that all but a very few who courageously fought that war are now retired. It seemed to me we were, for the first time, accepting the present.

To various degrees we Americans had been resting on our reputation for being innovative, resourceful, and hardworking. We had rejected any message from Japan that we were fooling ourselves. We had been like the patient who goes to his physician for X-rays. Then, not liking what he sees, he rejects surgery and employs a touchup artist to alter the X-rays.

President John F. Kennedy was a quarter of a century too early in his announcement that the torch had been passed. Now it has—but not before our arrogance peaked. Believing we could have guns and butter simultaneously and financing our longest war with a balloon note that incubated the staggering national debt of the 1980s, we had to try the touch-ups of a wage and price freeze, a grain embargo, a detrimental foreign practice act, a dagger-twisting period of inflation, and finally reality.

The New Economic Frontier

For the first time in thirty years of lecturing, I find audiences assenting to one of my basic premises: History is not cyclical. It may be coincidental, but it is false that the more things change, the more things are the same. History is not a Lionel train around the Christmas tree. Each experience teaches us that lessons are not repeated. E. H. Carr observed that the writing of history had a dual and reciprocal function: "to promote our understanding of the past in the light of the present, and of the present in the light of the past."

As a lad I watched a slide screen as Bible teacher Dr. Isaac Pace showed us picture after picture of snowflakes. Each had a perfect center with symmetrical balance, but none were alike. I was convinced then that if the God of this universe never duplicates Himself or His creations, then dissimilar affairs of mankind can never yield a cyclical result. I agree with Nobel prize winner Herbert Simon that human behavior cannot be logically defined. Because human beings are infinitely diverse, so their conduct will be also.

The curse of cyclical thinking gives us the phrase, "Hang in there." Ostensibly meant as a phrase of encouragement, it has come to mean, "If you just endure long enough, the good times will return. Don't take any action of your own. Don't think, dream, or plan. Just wait! Things always get better!"

The flip side of that fantasy is the conscientious executive who can't figure how to do more, yet the favorable results (compared to those of the generation before) seem elusive.

Today's leader faces a new economic frontier. The resources at his or her disposal are lean. The window that was open to the generation before has been slammed shut.

The window? Well, we conveniently forget that from 1945 to 1955 the United States controlled half of the world's acknowledged wealth. We hadn't earned nor yearned for such a lofty position. We were fortunate that not one World War II bomb had dropped on the then forty-eight continental states. We were a generation before the jet-shrinking of the oceans. We had also proven again that no group can fight as courageously as a people dedicated to peace who only will accept war as a last alternative. We entered the war in 1941 as a young nation suffering an inferiority complex, and we emerged victorious less than four years later as the banker of the world.

Inferiority complex? Yes, that is what it was. Following the stock market crash of '29, we fully entered the Great Depression. The whole civilized world was depressed, but with limited communications, that was little comfort. We felt we alone had frustrated our forebears' dream of a promised land. We alone had refuted the economic premises of Adam Smith. Embarrassed, we went through the denial stage of saying, "All we have to fear is fear itself." Then we grasped for a quick-fix potion mixed by a British economist, John Maynard Keynes. That, we thought, would at least arrest the problem. But to many of us the second wave in 1938 carried underneath it a more severe tidal wave. A third of our workers were unemployed; gas cost 3.85 cents per gallon. The Depression that eased in our northern states but not in the South until 1943 was finally cured by the most radical medicine of all, World War II.

The generation of leaders just before the war faced a never-to-be-repeated decade. From 1929 to 1941 the Depression curbed domestic buying. Soup lines, not fashion lines, made the headlines. From 1941 to 1945 the money began to flow but was channeled into shipyards, tanks being built at auto plants, and rivets for Rosie to use on plane wings.

We conquered our enemies and then had to address a

nation with full purses and not much to spend the money on for sixteen years. No wonder there was a waiting list for anything our predecessors made in the late 1940s and early 1950s, from a matchbox for a house to an inverted bathtub for a car. People clamoring to regain their place in the sun spun the revolving doors of our stores. The one-dimensional use of technology to win a war was now loosed to support the creativity of the private sector.

Bigger had to be better.

Needed: Leaders to Guide a Debtor Nation

Gospel was written on the premise that what was good for General Motors was good for the world.

In 1964 I was literally booed by Dr. Floyd Bond's MBA candidates at the University of Michigan when I was brazen enough to suggest that the challenge of their careers might be to know when not to grow. No, I was not suggesting the other extreme that "small is beautiful," but I was convinced it was time to restore temperance and discipline to our behavior pattern.

We are not in a cycle. The post-World War II window has been slammed shut and barred. The cavalry ain't comin' for the horses have come up lame in impassable terrain. Leadership loneliness has become the executive's "in" disease. Those who know what is going on are not planning for the year 2000 or the twenty-first century, but for tomorrow, a "today at a time."

Am I discouraged? Quite the contrary. It is refreshing to witness the new reality where phoniness, hype, and fakery are burned out. In my view, an executive search is aborning to find out, "warts and all," if leadership exists. From Socrates we are relearning that "the unexamined life is not worthy of being lived."

The frontiers are not reached or closed. On my desk someone placed the following: "Large areas of our inheritance are unsown, unreaped; all kinds of beginnings abide sorrowfully incomplete. We live in the strange land of the undone." These

20

frontiers defy the tired blood of the knowledgeable pessimist or the giddiness of the tranquilized optimist.

Our fathers managed surpluses. We are looking for leaders to guide a debtor nation. That's right—the nation that banked the world now owes the world. What Wendell Wilkie, B. C. Forbes, Marshall McLuhan, and other internationalists were unable to teach us, our economics are forcing us to face. We have shuttles around the world but have not lived in the world. Charles Dudley Walker feels that "isolation breeds conceit."

On the evening of July 3, 1986, I stood as the guest of the Coca Cola Company for the rededication of "Lady Liberty." We were called to remember, renew, and rejoice. As I applauded the Statue of Liberty's new dress and alluring face-lift, I realized we were not celebrating our independence, but our interdependence. We, who to some degree had accepted being our brother's keeper, are now having to adjust to being kept by our brothers.

It has been suggested that World War II gave definition to management, and I, for one, honor the level of efficiency American managers have reached. Yet there is a dearth of leadership. Unfortunately, we have made the titles interchangeable. Most leaders can manage, but few managers can lead.

We manage tangibles, whether persons or things, that already exist. The leader is responsible for having the vision and the energy to lead people from the nonexistent to existence. Like Einstein, the leader covets an ability to comprehend the obvious. Why is grass really green?

For instruction in this leadership role (since there's no cavalry on the way), let's revisit the first frontiersman, pioneer, and pilgrim. His biography, fittingly enough, is found in the Genesis portion of God's kaleidoscope. His name is Abraham and he is called the father of us all. I am fortunate that my dad told me the story of Abraham when I was a lad, so that I developed early some expectations of the price one pays to lead.

Abraham's story from Genesis is summarized for us in Hebrews 11:8–16, which gives us three simple but sublime observations about leadership.

1. Abraham led even though he didn't know exactly where he was going.

"By faith Abraham obeyed when he was called to go out . . . . And he went out, not knowing where he was going" (v. 8). Abraham was a pathfinder.

He left from a place called Ur of the Chaldees. A two-letter city (Ur) doesn't sound like much, but archaeological research reveals it was a city with a generous harbor and patrician homes for its citizens. Abraham relinquished managing security and headed into a desert.

Leaders seek new directions and respect new approaches. (Note: I am writing about "pathfinders," not "pathfollowers.") Although he uses all the knowledge available to establish the direction, a leader doesn't always know where he's going. Don't minimize that leadership is a "walk by faith." The more I am briefed by financial analysts, the more privy I am to futuristic think tanks, the more I study demographics, the more I am convinced that the only person who can lead amidst these confusing signals is someone humble enough to walk out and lead by faith.

Two men come to mind: W. E. "Bill" LaMothe, chairman of Kellogg Company, and R. Gordon McGovern, president and CEO of Campbell Soup Company. They have quietly, but with tenacity, revolutionized the manufacturing process and productivity of their stately, old companies. In both cases, the companies were enjoying strong profits; so their actions were not reactions to the pressure of losses but rather cases of the good getting better. What they are doing cannot even be called "state of the art." It is pioneering, reminding me of that quatrain I learned in grade school years ago:

> *Thank God for fools—for men who dare to dream*
> *Beyond the lean horizon of their days;*
> *Men not too timid to pursue the gleam*
> *To unguessed lands of wonder and amaze.*

Twenty-five hundred years ago, the Chinese thinker, Lao-tzu, taught that leadership would be simple if we were moving straight forward in an extension of the past, so we charted our path by yesterday's markers. But the ancient thinker said that ambiguity and surprise are in our future. Intuition, experience, emotions, and gut reactions identify the leader.

Life is full of good surprises when the path we take is not perfectly paved. In 1975 I responded to a crisis in the national office of the Boy Scouts of America. I received an offer of help from a concerned Texan. (Some people are unaware that Scouting is the largest nongovernmental youth agency in the free world with an annual budget exceeding $175 million.)

H. Ross Perot, the man offering to help us address one of our major problems, was the fellow who, in 1962, while selling for IBM, became convinced that the computer industry's value to all of us would be enhanced if it provided a complete package of services—hardware, software, and advice weren't enough. IBM didn't share his vision.

On his thirty-second birthday, with $1,000 in his pocket, Ross started his own business. Twenty-one years later he sold his business to General Motors for $2.5 billion. He personally made $1.2 billion!

Ross found a path and began to lead others. Visions can't be taught. They have to be sought—and at the beginning are usually expensive.

2. *Abraham lived by high standards at all times in all circumstances.*

As I was leaving for college, my dad gave me a benediction: "Remember, son, God is more interested in *you* than anything you'll do, but whatever you do, do it well, for you never know when God is standing in the shadows measuring you for a bigger opportunity."

The Bible states that Abraham sojourned. He was an adventurer. The word *sojourn* has the meaning of a side trip, unplanned and undirected. There is romance in leadership, but like all matters of love, there is a price. The leader pays the price that reduces the cost to his followers. The payoff comes when effective leadership broadens the horizon.

John Gardner wrote in his classic work *Self Renewal* (New York: Harper and Row, 1964):

> Exploration of the full range of his own potentialities is not something that the self-renewing man [leader] leaves to the chances of life. It is something he pursues systematically, or at least avidly, to the end of his days. He looks forward to an endless and unpredictable dialogue between his potentialities and the claims of life—not only the claims he encounters but the claims he invents. And by potentialities I mean not just skills but the full range of his capacities for sensing, wondering, learning, understanding, loving and aspiring.

The leader's continued internal growth and stamina hinges upon not looking back nor walking sideways. When the pioneers left St. Louis, there was no returning. Of Abraham, Hebrews 11:15–16 reads: "And truly if they had called to mind that country from which they had come out, they would have had opportunity to return. But they now desire a better, that is, a heavenly country."

No, I'm not hinting that the leader is too stubborn to admit the path is wrong, nor am I giving comfort to the intractable. Such are not leaders, for childishness is never better illuminated than by arrogance. I am saying leadership goes forward without reciting yesterday's accomplishments or taking refuge in nostalgia when the winds rise.

Henry David Thoreau believed, "If one advances confidently in the direction of his dreams, and endeavors to live the life which he has imagined, he will meet with a success unexpected in common hours." One may manage by the clock, but adventuresome leadership is a commitment to life.

3. Abraham was a leader because he kept preparing in spite of not knowing exactly the what, the when, or the how.

Did any of our early pioneers envision today's West? No. Nor could childless Abraham imagine how God would make his heirs as many as the stars of the heaven and the sands of the seashore.

We say leaders are to see the big picture, but if the picture is only as big as the leader can see, then the dimensions are too small to be lasting. You never hear a leader speak of his success because, like wealth, if it can be measured, it isn't success. Pathfinders look not for destination but for destiny. Abraham died never knowing whether he had arrived—nor did he inquire.

Little wonder that three different times in the Bible Abraham is called "a friend of God." A friend is esteemed above others, someone we love and feel loved by, someone with whom we find mental compatibility and in whom we have trust and confidence. The Bible does not grant perfection to Abraham. He had his mental, moral, and physical collapses. His days of duplicity in Egypt were embarrassing. But on the balance he was a friend of God because he accepted what God can do through any of us despite our limitations.

Without a cavalry to rescue us, without a simple solution to complex problems, the lonely leader may find that inspiration comes only with the assurance that God plus one always makes a majority.

In the spring of 1986 the newspapers carried the obituary of Tenzing Norgay. This Sherpa peasant from the Himalayan town of Darjeeling was the personal aide to Sir Edmund P. Hillary. Norgay was with the famous New Zealander when he scaled the 29,000-foot Mount Everest. On the climb they realized the remains of another British expedition that had failed thirty years before was buried there. Indeed, Sir Edmund himself had futilely tried before. On May 29, 1953, the two men were approaching the pinnacle. Below, the news media were focusing on them through their telescopic lenses. Even then the climbers appeared as little dots, barely visible through the snow mists swirling about them. Just before they laid claim to the top, a cloud cover enveloped them. One of the writers filed this headline with his wire story:

Hillary Last Seen Reaching Toward the Peak

So, like the wagonmasters of the Old West, leaders begin their odyssey reaching, never knowing or caring if they arrive. The promise and the perils of the path move them.

2

Snowcapped Rockies . . .
Parched Plains . . .
Untamed Rivers . . .
Scorching Deserts . . .

Sir Oliver Wright has served Her Majesty's government in the United States for forty years. Beginning as a vice-consul in New York City in 1946, he rose to the office of Ambassador of Great Britain to the United States. In his farewell address delivered to the Town Hall of California, May 20, 1986, he reviewed his feelings about Americans:

> . . . whole families would set off in wagons at the first thaw of spring and hope to get to the Pacific, by the Oregon or Santa Fe trails, before winter set in. It is a wonderful story. This "can do" spirit leads to a conviction that all problems are soluble. Just throw enough energy, intelligence, money and good will at a problem and a solution can be found. The immediate American reaction to a problem is "C'mon fellers, let's go," sometimes, it seems to me, without too much thought of where they're going or what they will do when they get there. *British and other sourpusses have been known to mutter under their breath, "Cowboys."*

It has been suggested by many that "the West" is more a mindset to Americans than a geographic location. Our early pioneers were not unlike Abraham of old. They moved far more by promises than by experiences. By definition, *frontier* carries the idea of the unknown.

We forget that many of the early pioneers could not speak English and for a very good reason. They were new not only to

26

the West but to the whole country. Emigrating from Scandinavia or Central Europe, many were lured by the promises that what they could find out West was "just like home." A day out of St. Louis they knew that was wrong.

In the snowcapped mountains, parched plains, untamed rivers, and scorched deserts, they found little resemblance to the quiet, tamed, well-manicured farms of their fathers. The people, the customs, the laws, the land were a cultural shock beyond preparation. These pioneers were starting over. They wouldn't turn back. They simply wanted *leadership* to show them how to claim the land, and that leadership could come only from within their group.

Ah, there is the problem of the frontier, no matter what the generation or location. Who will lead? Who knows the way? Where have all the leaders gone? Where do leaders come from?

Unraveling the Mystique of Leadership

Historians estimate that when the United States began, there were sixty leaders out of a population of three million people, or one leader for every fifty thousand souls. A couple of dozen come to mind—Washington, Jefferson, Franklin, John and Sam Adams, Lafayette, Tom Paine, Patrick Henry. If my mathematics are right, we should have 4,500 leaders today. Can you name one hundred? Do you believe we have 4,500? Leadership is a rare quality that does not spring from fame, prestige, or wealth. Those are simply the tributes and rewards we might bestow as an acknowledgment of the leaders' greatness.

In my travels throughout the United States at the rate of a thousand miles a day, speaking once a day for twenty-five years, I've been rewarded with a significant blessing. I've come to know leaders whose hands I've been able to shake, whose eyes I've been able to look into, and whose character I've grown to appreciate.

Unraveling the mystique of leadership is not easy. The footprints in the sands of time do get scuffed. No formula or curricula of studies exist to divulge their secrets. Great leaders are much like electrical current: we are aware of their power even though we do not understand how they work. It is no wonder, then, that in ancient times, great leaders were deified by men—if not by Zeus. Upon their deaths, people all too often were left with Shakespeare's classic line on the death of Caesar, "Whence comes such another?"

But leadership is not an ordination by so-called gods. Though some men and women have more talent for it than others, leadership is both understandable and learnable. It begins with the ageless question of which comes first, the chicken or the egg? Are there leaders hanging around waiting for a challenge? Or, are there challenges waiting for someone to break out of the pack and become a leader? Would Bill Travis or Davy Crockett have been famous without an Alamo? The answer may be a combination of both.

My friend Guy Carr, one of North Carolina's most decorated Army officers during World War II, had no goal of being dynamic or heroic, but he honed his talents when he answered the call to the colors. He felt honored to serve his country. The bloody beaches of South Africa and Italy uncovered his latent leadership abilities.

God forbid that we have any more world wars to develop leaders, for as Einstein told us, if we have World War III, then World War IV will be fought with clubs and hatchets.

Still, one of the problems facing today's youth is that they haven't had a defined way to be tested—neither war nor depression. None of us knows much about ourselves until we face the loss of our lives or our possessions or our reputations. Suicide statistics on young people are moving off the chart and drugs have become common crutches because the youth of this country have found no adequate test to know who they are or what they possess within themselves.

Even in the life of Jesus, before His leadership was recognized publicly, He was tested on three grounds, according to Matthew 4:1-11:

1. *The Physical Test.* "If You are the Son of God, command that these stones become bread." Jesus answered, "It is written, 'Man shall not live by bread alone, but by every word that proceeds from the mouth of God.' " To put it crudely, lead-

ership is not brute strength; it is finesse. It is not dictatorial; it is directional. It is not the survival of self; it is service to others.

2. The Power Test.   Next, the Bible tells us, "The devil took Him up into the holy city, set Him on the pinnacle of the temple, and said to Him, 'If You are the Son of God, throw Yourself down. For it is written: "He shall give His angels charge concerning you." ' " Since the devil quoted the Bible, so did Jesus: "You shall not tempt the LORD your God."

Phillips Brooks was called "the Prince of Boston." Actually, he was senior pastor of Holy Trinity Church, ministering to the city's upscale business community. A reporter wrote: "On the darkest of days when Phillips Brooks walked down Boylston Street, the sun had to shine." To the laity of his congregation he suggested:

> Don't pray for easy tasks. Pray for stronger men. Don't pray for tasks equal to your power. Pray for power equal to your tasks. Then the doing of your work shall be no miracle, but you, yourself, shall be a miracle.

Leadership is not garnering power. Leadership is the stewardship of power.

3. The Prosperity Test.   On the last temptation, "the devil took Him up on an exceedingly high mountain, and showed Him all the kingdoms of the world and their glory. And he said to Him, 'All these things I will give You if You will fall down and worship me.' Then Jesus said to him, 'Away with you, Satan! For it is written, "You shall worship the LORD your God, and Him only you shall serve.' "

The prosperity test asks whether you want the romance of being honored or the agonies, the pains, the disciplines, and the scars that leadership imposes. The closing verse of this passage may say it all: "Then the devil left Him, and behold, angels came and ministered to Him." Such ministering may come to all who pass the physical test, the power test, and the prosperity test and thus are ready for the mantle of leadership.

The Qualities of True Leaders

The preceding biblical lesson is cited not to prove that as a former parish minister I can still outline a sermon or homily but to establish that I am writing about true leaders, not just heads of companies.

Maybe President Calvin Coolidge overstated the case when he said, "The business of America is business," but not by much, for the business statesman has been on the very frontier of our growth. The men and women cited in this book are in that category, and I name them even though my doing so might embarrass them in the midst of their leading.

It is easy enough to describe the characteristics of a leader. E. F. Gerard put it succinctly: "Leadership is achieved by ability, alertness, experience and keeping posted; by willingness to accept responsibility; a knack for getting along with people; an open mind and a head that stays clear under stress."

Admirable, sounds good, not too common, but not too rare either. But Gerard's definition is much like a description of the horses entered in the Kentucky Derby, the Preakness, or the Belmont Stakes. Each horse is a winner of preliminary races in California or Florida. But a Triple Crown winner has all these winning attributes plus a rare, vital difference: *the heart* of the leader.

Benjamin Hoff, applying the teachings of Lao-tzu to *Winnie the Pooh* in the *Tao of Pooh* (New York: Dutton, 1982), wrote: "The masters of life [the leaders] . . . know the way. They listen to the voice within them, the voice of wisdom and simplicity, the voice that reasons beyond cleverness and knows beyond knowledge. " No wonder Jesus taught that those who are converted must be *childlike*, although not childish.

Now, let's jump forward centuries from Lao-tzu. Imagine yourself a historian in 2076 and, assuming the United States is still standing, you are trying to identify the most important achievement during the last quarter of our twentieth century. Would you write about microchips, space conquest, biotechnology, genetic engineering, AIDS, or TV evangelism? I believe I would write about the business executives who, in the strength of Gideon's minority, became heroes.

Called by God to free Israel from the control of the Midianites, Gideon proceeded to do so with a huge host of people, only to be told by God that only he himself with a few of the elect would be needed for the job.

The Gideon "few" I write about know that the vagaries of politics do not endanger their efforts. They measure themselves not on where they are pegged on the *Forbes* or *Fortune* "Hit Parade," but on their changing things. While their business peers look for excuses to justify poor earnings, these "few" executives are finding jobs they enjoy; while their peers bemoan new problems with new names, these "few" accept problems with honest realism, joying in the challenge of risk.

Writing from our imaginary position in 2076, we will remember that these business-hero leaders were not created in the 1970s or 1980s but were always at the foundation of our progress. Thus, much of our time is spent in identifying and praising those leaders who believe they only fully sense their worth when the elements defy them.

Speaking to a group of executives, Daniel K. Frierson of Dixie Yarns Corporation quoted Thomas Jefferson to the effect that "To be independent in the comforts of life we must fabricate them ourselves. Manufacturers are now as necessary to our independence as to our comforts." But, concluded Dan, "*Unnatural* it is to expect yesterday's solutions to solve today's problems. It is just wrong thinking to take comfort that any trend is indefinite. It is a *trend . . .* only a trend."

Alexis de Tocqueville, spending the 1830s and 1840s observing the American scene, devoted an entire chapter of *Democracy in America* to the extreme scarcity of lofty ambitions among otherwise intensely ambitious Americans. He felt this to be our striking paradox: we strongly encourage individual development, yet, we debunk our heroes and resent greatness. Maybe we want our heroes and their greatness to be so authentic that they must get up off the mat after we take our best shot. We want to be sure we are being given a vision and not a mere apparition.

Sure, as a lad I had my fictional heroes: Tom Mix delivered me from the Indians; Jack Armstrong made me the toughest kid on the block; Captain Midnight gave me the secret message so I could locate the spies. They were my Luke Skywalkers, Indiana Joneses, and Rambos. I'm grateful that my parents and teachers balanced my entertainment with required reading about our business leaders. Biographical reading let me know early on that Anatole France was correct when he observed that we were saved by our magnificent "madmen." I only appreciated their genius in subsequent reflection. Henry Fairlie speaks for me when he says, "A hero is not just someone we admire. He is someone whom we idealize. A hero has some very definite attributes of his own, but it is we who give a special significance to them." Those I look to today become embarrassed if I suggest they are larger than life, but their attractiveness is their practice of leadership.

Yet they are real. Like in all of us, there may be hidden away in them the jolly old slob who likes putting on multi-washed jeans, the ratty college team jersey, the ripped sneakers with the big toe sticking out. The periodic break in routine is essential as we'll see later, but it cannot be the pattern. Leaders and heroes always carry the flag. They may even *be* the flag. Though, like all of us, they become sick, emotionally distressed, disappointed, and discouraged, they bear the burden silently, for they must not let their temporary weakness become a spreading virus among the followers.

Does leadership sound like a pretty high calling? It is. It is *not* for everyone.

The Birth of Navistar

An example of a leader and a very mature company moving efficiently into the new economic environment is Navistar. Navistar is not mirroring the shrink-to-survive mentality gripping too many companies, but instead has adapted a "change to compete" strategy. A Navistar ad appearing in *The Wall Street Journal* on July 23, 1986, contained this copy:

WE HAD A STRONG MOTIVATION TO EMBRACE
CHANGE
Change is frightening. It can paralyze powerful executives. It can cause entire organizations to drag their corporate feet. It's the stuff sleepless nights are made of.

Not long ago, International Harvester was in the shadow of an even more frightening prospect. The reaper was already at our doorstep. We had to change. Or else. We had to streamline operations. Greatly improve productivity. And find new ways to compete. The fact that you're reading this today is testimony to how well our people rally to change. We consolidated facilities. Eliminated five levels of bureaucracy. Doubled manufacturing productivity. Cut inventory by two-thirds. And orchestrated the largest private debt restructuring in history. An old company, set in its ways, changed. And was reborn as Navistar International Corporation. In doing so, we learned a lesson. Change is not a nemesis. It is vital to our organization. To any organization. Properly managed, change is progress. It's the road to improved quality, and to new products that will help our customers meet their changing needs. It's a competitive edge. Change helps us further strengthen our number one position. Yet we know we must never change merely for the sake of change. Change is not a goal. It's the means to a goal. Today, we're still changing. We're growing. Improving. And finding better ways to serve our customers. Change, however, still keeps us awake at night. But these days it's because we're dreaming of new ways to accomplish it.

International Harvester was an enigma. It had one of the most recognized names in U.S. industry, but was one of the more poorly managed companies during the 1970s. When the board, led by Bill Karnes and interim chairman Lou Menk, reached out and recruited Don Lennox, all they could promise him was the David-Goliath potential, meaning the problem was so giant that Don couldn't miss it.

Don's achieving career of nineteen years at Ford followed by a decade at Xerox entitled him to a luxurious retirement. But a new challenge can reverse aging. It was a good thing Bill and Lou couldn't describe how big Goliath was.

IH's troubles were not created by a miscalculated strike from November 1979 to the end of April 1980. That was just "the straw." For twenty years before, IH had paid stockholders too high a dividend level, depleting reinvestment funds for decaying plants. State-of-the-art machinery was never seriously considered.

Softness at the top quite naturally led to a pleasant place to work, but not a challenging place to work; so IH was a high-cost producer. IH didn't just match the labor settlements of the Big Three automobile companies; it bettered them. When the company reversed this practice in desperation, management didn't measure labor's determination to keep the gravy train running.

The company was losing $100 million a year in the construction division and had not made a profit in thirty years. Even a child would say the proof was there that IH couldn't run a construction business. Yet, management led the board to invest even more money in new and beautiful construction products—great to look at but too costly to buy. With an ego that makes a corporation want to own everything, they were paying $22.50 an hour to make fasteners themselves when they could have bought all they wanted from companies paying $9.50 an hour.

Being managed and not led, IH couldn't change without a drastic housecleaning. So the cry came: "Out with failed executives; now, Don Lennox, save us!"

Don moved rapidly. He was sympathetic, but innocent employees were about to suffer because of decisions they had not had a part in making. He moved before he became attached to faces and places. The workforce was reduced from 97,000 worldwide to 15,000 in the U.S. only!

The agriculture business that had started IH 150 years before was sold to Tenneco. Although some analysts said to hold on, Don faced the fact that the agriculture business was losing $1 million a day.

He had "sick moments" when he had to close the plant in Canton, Illinois—the only major employer for the town. Despite pressure from the mayor, clergy, governor, and secretary of agriculture, he couldn't turn back, although his heart went out to the 2,500 people now out of work.

Don gathered about him his three to four key executives, and together they decided what was essential to keep and essential to close. Challenges and decisions came fast and furiously: should they keep plants open in Australia, New Zealand, Mexico, South Africa? No! Do we need all these U.S. plants? No. Surplus plants in Wagoner, Oklahoma, Fort

Wayne, Indiana, Louisville, Kentucky, closed. They would sell what they could. Still, the write-down of "non-needed" meant a $1.6 billion loss in 1982. Within days of bankruptcy, Jim Cotting, Vice Chairman of Finance, designed an unprecedented creative refinancing without any mention of a government bail-out.

From the residue, Navistar was created. Although a much smaller company, it moved rapidly to a number one position in the combined medium and heavy truck market. The dealers are partners and no longer treated in a cavalier manner.

Visiting with Don Lennox one senses he recognized the dangers of his new frontier, but he had years before passed the physical test, the power test, the popularity test. He has more than the attributes of the leader. He has the *heart* of a mature leader who has not moved far from the advice all of us received as children: "If it's worth doing, it's worth doing right." Not almost right, not comparatively right, but right.

America Needs Courageous Business Leaders

Our nation turns to business leadership for realism and promise.

Stanley Gault, chairman of Rubbermaid, Inc., tells us that in 1889 the National Association of Manufacturers was organized in Cincinnati. There weren't that many manufacturers, but the call went out: "Come meet with us and we together will find out how to save this system and this society that has so much potential. We must commit ourselves as businessmen." Business took upon itself what government seemed impotent to do: to make this nation into a peaceful, tranquil, livable society with opportunity for all people to grow.

The late John Eagan who founded American Cast Iron Pipe Company and died too young in his midfifties, was eulogized by Dr. W. W. Alexander, Farm Security administrator, in the August 9, 1924 issue of *The Asheville Citizen:*

> John Eagan was probably the most remarkable businessman the South had produced since the [Civil] War; the forerunner of the new business man, who tired of just making money, had a restlessness to serve.

I have met with no other so conscientiously and devotedly determined to make his life something of use to as many others as possible. He was not thinking of amassing more money, or acquiring greater power, or enjoying selfishly more of the good things of life. Rather, his constant thought expressed in every action was that he felt his full responsibility for the proper use of his opportunities and wealth.

John J. Eagan of yesterday reminds me of the leaders, chronicled in this book. Their lives, as we have seen and will continue to see, can be summed up in this quotation years ago in *The Atlanta Constitution:* "John Eagan is a man of infinite courage, very gentle, very considerate, very kind—but *very firm.*"

Firmness gives credibility to the other attributes. The gentle heart leads across obstacles only if it is also the strong heart. Crossing snowcapped Rockies . . . parched plains . . . untamed rivers . . . scorching deserts means developing a strategy, suffering, and using defeats as course markers. No "wilting morning glories" need apply.

3

Where Have All the Buffalo Gone?

As the pioneers started their Western trek, they soon learned they could only take basic supplies. They knew they soon would have to live off the land, which meant learning the Indians' survival skills yet retaining their own identity.

The Indians of the Western plains were blessed with two assets that made them invincible until almost the dawn of this century. The first asset was the horse, introduced by the Spanish in the late 1500s. Having no word for "horse," yet appreciating the animal's great strength, loyalty, and beauty, the Indians seized upon the only similitude they knew: the dog. But the grace and speed of the horse made it much more than a dog; it was more akin to the gods, and so the animal was called sacred or god dog.

In fifty years the Indians so completely mastered the technique of horsemanship that General George Crook was moved to call them the "finest light cavalry the world has ever known." Their tactics in battle were never equaled by the U.S. Cavalry.

The second asset of the Indians was that moving meat market called the buffalo, the American bison. It provided not only nourishment, but clothing, shelter, weaponry, and tools. In fact, the buffalo was so central to the life and culture of the Indians that General Crook, considered the most competent Indian-fighter of his time, based his strategy for defeating them on the animal.

Crook knew his troopers could never tactically outfight the

mounted Indian, but because the Indian never learned to raise or pen the buffalo, he reasoned that if the herd could be destroyed, the Indian menace would come to an end.

The general was never allowed to carry out this plan, but it was, nevertheless, sound. The Indians thought the buffalo was an inexhaustible larder. Ironically, it was the Indians themselves, under the leadership of the Sioux Chief, Sitting Bull, who killed the last thousand head of bison remaining in southwestern Dakota in 1883.

The Difference Between Tactics and Strategy

Tactics win battles, but strategy wins wars. No less a person than Winston Churchill noted that the Germans in World War II were expert in small unit tactics, but never understood strategy.

To my dismay, I question if many American businessmen understand strategy either. They constantly seem to confuse it with tactics, insisting that every new product or merchandising idea is a new corporate strategy when it really is simply a new tactic.

Tactics are to efficient action as strategy is to effective action. Let me explain. In war, efficient action is trying to capture Bastogne as quickly as possible with the least loss of men and equipment. Effective action would be to bypass the town and continue to drive to the sea.

Efficiency-driven firms accomplish goals with a minimum of expense and energy. Efficiency is easy to understand: you work harder, more cheaply and more quickly than your competition; when all else fails you work longer hours. In tough times, you cut back on everything because that is efficient. However, the inadequacy of efficiency alone gives me opportunity to repeat my basic economic maxim:

You economize for efficiency but you sell for prosperity.

As you get more experienced in your field or your product matures in the marketplace, you simply get more efficient in making and servicing it. With this kind of tactical efficiency, results are realized much more quickly and there certainly is less risk. You become comfortable in the knowledge that you are working in the marketplace as you have always done, and your profit curve keeps rising—at least for the near term. What is wrong with that? Nothing, but if you haven't been doing any strategic thinking, you may be eating your last buffalo, your cash cow, or your seed corn.

Many U.S. companies wind up making the best and cheapest buggy whips ever, and sales managers are berating their sales staffs for sluggish sales, demanding to know why! Buggy whips may be a little harsh. Try steel or automobiles or VCRs or TV sets or clothing. . . .

Replacing Phony Strategic Planning with Real Strategic Planning

While tactics are concerned with *how* we accomplish goals, strategic planning is centered on *what* the goals are. Corporations are taking a hard look at strategic planning. They sense that the buffalo herd is getting thin. Intuitively, they know their present plans are short-lived. But I am surprised how few companies know what constitutes strategic planning.

Still I see corporations that feel the answer is to buy up tactical firms like themselves, thinking a greater market share with reduced competition will preserve the present product mix. This is really compounding the problem, and the strategic answer is further buried.

More common, it seems to me, are the companies that look West while the sun is still bright, thus getting sunspots and seeing mirages on the horizon. Such mirages run the gamut from reindustrialization to restructuring; from junk bonds to Chapter 11; from hostile takeovers to schemed alliances; from management by objectives to pay for performance; from walk-around to touchy-feely managing; from consultants to corporate planners; from Theory Z to back-to-basics; from autocratic bosses to demassing; from economists to executive celebrities; from synergy to corporate culture; from the Yuppies to the 50+ market. Mirages and fads —all with good features if they could be real and captured.

Can it be that strategic planning is too tough? Too realistic? Too unromantic? Too revealing? Most claim to have it in their corporations, but few really do. All CEOs want to feel it is being accomplished, but they refuse their personal leadership and time commitment to do it right.

What do I mean by strategic planning? It is entrepreneurial leadership; you may use the buzz word "intrapreneur" if you wish. I am in admiration, not of the inventor of a new product as much as the leader who rejuvenates a mature industry.

I'm aware of the new businesses being incorporated every day, but I'm addressing the vitality of the business establishment upon which so many of the new ventures depend for their niche.

Colin Stokes is a name that I will not let be forgotten from industry. He moved into the CEO office of R. J. Reynolds—a little cash cow—and saw a narrowing use of tobacco. He did what few people have the humility to do when they reach his level—that is, *admit what he didn't know*. He reached out and recruited J. Paul Sticht to strategize the turning of RJR into an aggressive, consumer-driven company. Paul, in turn, surrounded himself with creative marketers such as Ed Horrigan, Mike Miles, Fernando Gumucio, Jack Powers. This became the foundation of what we know today as RJR Nabisco.

Strategic planning is found in the corporation with much at risk that selects the right action at the right time. It is believing that the harder I work and the less I scheme, the better my luck is. Louis Pasteur taught, "Chance favors the prepared mind."

Strategic planning, therefore, is planning while being reluctant to predict.

Historian Sir Kenneth Clarke cautioned, "Predicting the future is, intellectually, the most disreputable form of public utterance." Or, as movie maker Sam Goldwyn is supposed to have said, "Never make predictions—especially about the future." Effective planning, at best, only offers greater reward because it entails greater risk.

Strategic planning is not crisis management. A crisis may

remind the company of the terrible omission of adequate planning, but a strategy is best developed when times are lush, when there are breathing spaces and dreaming moments. It means backing away from the day-to-day concerns and viewing the company's role in the larger picture of business life, both U.S. and global.

Strategic planning also is not accomplished by executives sitting encircled around an outside facilitator to bring out what we already know about each other and the business.

Alan Schriesham, Director of Argonne National Laboratory, addressing the American Power Conference in Chicago on April 14, 1986, asked if they were familiar with the Seersucker Theory published in 1980 by an associate professor at Wharton. The Seersucker Theory says that in a given field, the average expert makes a better forecaster than a layman. However, the expert is only marginally better than the average student. Most companies do not need expert help for the far out future nor interpreters of the historic past.

What is needed is positioning your company for today. This is best done by mobilizing the people responsible for your company's behavior. The Seersucker Theory describes the attitude of companies that believe there is outside wisdom anxiously waiting to formulate their planning. The Wharton school calls this "seersucker" because there is no such seer, only a sucker to pay for one. We cannot take the plan or process that has been successful in one organization and expect the same results from giving it to another company. Each company has its own personality and idiosyncrasies.

Bill Dearden: The Fulfillment of Milton Hershey's Prophecy

No person better illustrates the use of strategic planning than Bill Dearden, CEO of Hershey Corporation. Born to a working-class family and raised by a single parent, Bill was the beneficiary of Milton Hershey's devotion to education. Bill became a student at Hershey Schools. Little did anyone know he was to be the fulfillment of Milton Hershey's prophecy. After Mr. Hershey had made and lost a fortune—and made it again—he was asked by a reporter if he ever regretted placing his wealth in an irrevocable trust to raise orphans. He and Mrs. Hershey were childless. With a twinkle in his eye, Mr. Hershey responded that he just knew someday, some under-privileged kid would come to Hershey Schools and go on to head the corporation. Bill Dearden fulfilled that dream.

After finishing Hershey Schools, Bill accepted scholarships to Albright College, Temple University, and Harvard Business School. Bill was employed by Dun and Bradstreet when he was called into military service. Upon discharge, he was asked to return to Hershey Schools and assist the business side. His tremendous sense of debt to the Hershey family led him to accept the position at financial sacrifice. His talent was imme-diately recognized and four years later he became assistant to the chairman of the Hershey Corporation. Often, as I visit with leaders, I find that, like Bill, they take an apparent step backward to move forward.

Freighted with devotion and a sense of debt to Hershey, Bill, when he became president of Hershey, would have found it easiest to adopt a safe course of action and just preserve what he inherited; protect it from any ravages; make sure the company just remained solid and strong, keeping its heavy cash flowing. How could he risk letting his benefactor down?

Here is where the inheritor of a company proves whether he is a leader or a manager, an innovator or a caretaker.

Playing it safe was not Bill Dearden's style. He knew that the company had never done any advertising. Unique. They not only made chocolate for their use but for most of the other major candy companies. Again we see that history is not cyclical, for the day of chocolate monopoly was gone, never to return again.

Bill understood Mr. Hershey and knew that he had taken risks, and just preserving the status quo would not be protect-ing the business. Preserving the status quo would have failed the spirit of Milton S. Hershey. Bill decided that the best way to show his gratitude to Hershey was to test by venture, by probing, and by taking calculated risks. The new, aggressive advertising just became the bell cow of the new day. Bill had to be the one to say, "We can take no comfort from our historic past. We have the best name in the industry; we are respected in the marketplace, but none of this will help for tomorrow."

Becoming CEO, Bill initiated his formal strategic planning in July of 1976 while we as a country were celebrating the two-hundredth birthday of our independence. Bill led his team into ten formal planning sessions consisting of sixteen full days of work, plus homework. This action demonstrated an important maxim:

Strategic planning, to be strategic, must be led by the CEO and viewed as the most important function of the leader.

Bill was the *elan vital*. Neither cocky nor defiant, he resolutely set about to be the creative force within Hershey, producing the growth necessary for success. Bill firmly believed Peter Drucker's comment: "Planning tries to optimize tomorrow the trends of today. Strategy aims to exploit the new and unforeseen opportunities of tomorrow."

Bill's team began by formalizing a mission statement. The statement gave direction for the company and closed with these two paragraphs:

> To accomplish this we must establish and maintain the capabilities and reputation for operating as an astute company that locates the right opportunities and manages for growth.
> We will carry out the mission within the framework provided by the corporate strategic plan and the statement of corporate philosophy.

Since 13 was my athletic uniform number, it stood out in my mind that the Hershey executives developed thirteen corporate strategic objectives. The objectives covered growth, financial resources, marketing, management procedures, personnel recruitment and competence, technology, commodities, government relations, international posture, facilities, energy, productivity, and corporate responsibility.

Strategic Planning at Hershey Corporation

The benefits to Hershey, Bill told me, included:

1. Top leadership is forced to answer the question: "What do *we* want this business to be?" Not what will it be if we do nothing, or what will it be due to competition . . . government regulations . . . commodity costs . . . or other outside influences. Jack Webb in the old TV series *Dragnet* may have introduced such clarity with his oft-repeated line, "Just the facts, Ma'am."

2. Having decided who we are and what we want, our strategic plan then becomes the road map within a given time frame. A corporation can't "Amway Rally" itself into long-term achievement. Pep rallies are not synonymous with potency. The public realizes that "the louder I shout, the less certain I am." Business run like a tent meeting has the duration of one. With one voice the people cry, "You're not for real. You called upon us in the audience to become enthusiastic about an intellectual, logical, yet mystical challenge that is fueled by hard work. We have been bombarded by lecturers' loud braggadocio. They wanted us to give them a 'high' so they could forget their mediocrity at home."

The strategic plan or road map retains the Abraham mindset. It points a direction based on the best we can be today, but is not thought to be a panacea. "It doesn't," as Bill Dearden would say, "make your business decisions any easier to wrestle with, but it does narrow the sphere of your concentration and give you time to act on the most important."

The strategic plan prepares for the reality of the unseen. Detours are recognized as not only possible, but probable, whether they be inflation, commodity disarray, or an accident outside the domain. In fact, now that a map has been developed, if there are unreasonable detours, we still know our basic direction and can redraw the map to get around the sliding rocks.

3. Putting the plan together will allow us to understand and evaluate our team better. We encourage them to question even the sacrosanct of our company. We encourage their "stretchability" to formulate plans out of ambiguous ideas and concepts. We say, "I don't want to move forward without picking your brains for alternative

implications and approaches." By demonstrating our confidence in them, we send the clear message that an effective strategic plan must be aware of corporate culture, meaning the internal workings of the corporation, and must be compatible with the people employed.

Strategic planning is the finest compliment we can give our team. Some never do open planning because their egos make them feel that when they shave each morning, the board has met. Still, I admire the honesty of a fellow who, leading an organization, had a picture of the board of directors in the reception hall of his company: ten different poses of himself.

Remember, in strategic planning sessions, we are saying "I need you!" And as a young gold medal Olympian reported, "Four working in harmony of a goal is like the strength of twelve." In this way, strategic planning is contrasted with standards of performance. We are not just compiling a glossary of each person's intentions, but focusing their psychic power into a pragmatic plan.

The "proof of the pudding" is in Hershey's growth, in both profits and products. The proof of Bill Dearden's pudding was an increase of sales from $556 million and profits of $39.3 million when he took over to a mind-boggling $1.893 billion in sales with profits of $108.7 million when he retired.

Even more significant is that "the beat goes on," for when Bill retired, the team, led by Dick Zimmerman, still keeps moving on.

4. Strategic planning must widen the peripheral vision of the leaders so the team members can narrow their vision to scrutinizing and staring. The process is built on varying degrees of innovation, entrepreneurial risk, dynamism, and pragmatism, all homogenized by the leader.

Strategic planning is not a free-for-all. The leader must be the captain and stay involved totally. He must also define the restrictions so there can be release of freedom. Sound contradictory?

When I was a lad, my fun included flying kites. In the Depression, of course, we made our own kites from newspapers, the cross bows from pliable birch. The tail of the kite was from my mother's pre-World War II authentic silk hose, darned until she was sewing darns on darns. The string was captured from food packages, pieces tied together by square knots and wrapped around a stick until I had enough to get down to business. Then I waited for a brisk fall breeze.

As I ran across the meadow, letting my string out, and as the kite soared, I boasted, "Wright Brothers, wherever you are, bow in recognition of my contribution to aerodynamics!" Suddenly, to my dismay, one of my carefully tied square knots wasn't, and the *slip* knot slipped! Released, the kite flew out of sight. Right? Wrong! If you say it flew away, you never flew a kite. The kite found the nearest tree, and there ended my career as an aeronautical engineer. The very string that had looked as if it was holding the kite down was actually the force that had helped get the kite up. The leader wanting the best results knows:

The planning process must not be inhibited but restricted only enough so that each participant knows the released operating area. The resulting strategic plan will have the value and balance of restriction and release.

5. Energy, enthusiasm and, yes, entrepreneurship are the results of the strategic planning.

Let me share a quotation and a statement I use often in speeches. A German business writer observed, "When I visit the United States, I see all the same faces as CEOs. All they have done is change their address."

The followers' security is in proportion to the strength they assign to the leader.

How are these two statements related? We like to blame all of our economic failing on outside circumstances and forces, but this is wrong. Golden Parachutes, stock options, and intemperate perks have given us the fast-track breed: one who takes over the company, pumps up the stock, since that has a direct bearing on his incentive bonus, and then waits for the takeover, enhancing himself even if it hurts the company. Finally, he sells the corporation at its inflated number, moments before the balloon bursts. Such have no need of strategic planning, but rather would have their plans "corrupted" by effective planning. This may be the ultimate white-collar crime.

Strategic planning, instead, commits us to the long term. It lets the associates know that they can trust their best contributions to our stewardship. That still doesn't mean we can jump in quickly and push the "on" button for planning. Bill Dearden would verify that there is a start-up time until our associates sense our seriousness in hanging the future of the corporation on the results of the sessions.

So we do not move gradually but put the full weight of what we desire to achieve right up front. Henry Thoreau said: "In the long run, men hit only what they aim at. Therefore, though they should fail immediately, they had better aim high."

At the same time, strategic planning doesn't relieve the leader of the loneliness built into his position. Henry Mohr reminds us, "You've heard it before, everybody has said it, the generals in the war have said it. Sometimes it's kind of lonely at the top." The colonels help formulate the strategy, but the beginning resolve and the final decision rest at the top.

Our milieu today—whether a corporation, school, association, or church—is fast-moving, constantly changing, and dynamic. For the organization wanting to share the future, observation of the horizon must be met with courageous ideas. We cannot afford to say, "If it ain't broke, don't fix it." Instead, our slogan is, "If it's working well, we'll seek to make it better." We must be responsive to today's needs. Today's achievements and tomorrow's accomplishments result from ideas properly clothed. If the leader, no matter how astute, turns inward, he may define the potential changes and innovations too narrowly.

We must avoid, if possible, crisis management. Far better to share our best thinking, anticipating our consumers' needs and wants. We must be willing to cast aside yesterday's methods, however effective, for those designed for tomorrow. This requires risk-taking and leaving old ground, no matter how sacred. It was not easy for Bill Dearden to move out on the frontier territory that Milton Hershey never even knew existed.

Yet, we cannot be reckless pioneers. According to Luke, Jesus cautions us: "For which of you, intending to build a tower, does not sit down first and count the cost, whether he has enough to finish it—lest after he has laid the foundation, and is not able to finish it, all who see it begin to mock him. . . ."

We must plan strategically. We must critically analyze and evaluate what we see on the horizon. We must satisfy the desires of our constituency even though the innovation or change may cause us discomfort. We cannot conduct business as usual.

In 1986 I again had the privilege of being on the Food Marketing Institute (FMI) podium with Stanley Marcus of Neiman-Marcus fame. My favorite quotation of his for which I thank him again, he delivered as only he can: "There is no detail so small that *we* can afford to overlook it, nor any challenge so large that *we* are afraid to face it."

4

Fort by the River

It is difficult today to imagine the extreme personal hardships that the pioneers endured. Unwashed for weeks, hands and feet blistered, bruised, and cut, saddle sores unattended, skin parched by the never-ending prairie wind, hair dried like straw by the burning sun were only a few of their discomforts. Any real injury, whether caused by knife or cooking flame, could only be temporarily doctored, for the wagon train had to keep moving.

The only real breaks were the midday "noonin' " for lunch in the shade of a wagon bed and a few hours after dark when the cooking utensils had been cleaned and repacked for the morrow's journey—and, of course, Sundays, when anything to be fixed was patted and patched back to use for the coming week.

But of all the deprivations felt by men, women, and children, nothing was worse than the loss of conversation and commerce with other human beings outside the wagon train.

"Can you eat those funny-looking birds I saw? . . . What do you do for flavorin' when you run out of salt? . . . Aren't the Indians colorful? . . . You think they're all bad? . . . Do you have a preacher in your train?" These and thousands of other questions constantly posed themselves to the travelers with only the meager knowledge of the wagon master for answers.

Fort Laramie by the Platte River was not only balm for the weary but hope for the discouraged. There the pioneers could get washed, doctored, repaired, resupplied, and informed about the trail ahead. Fort Laramie was a storehouse of information for the men, a heaven of conversation for the women, and pure delight for the children. Even the animals seemingly sighed with relief as the wagons were unhitched and repaired.

Most of all, Fort Laramie was where they measured themselves, took inventory of their needs, and decided whether and when they could move out. They had reached almost a halfway point. Naiveté had been lost the first day on the trail. In its place had come a defiance, a determination that they could tame this good land. They were amused amidst the seriousness of their mission. They had to laugh when comparing what they had anticipated to what they experienced.

Is the new frontier of today any different? It was said of a minister that his sermons eloquently answered all the questions that no one was asking. So I feel in our preparation to do business we have procedures and we have problems, but the two haven't found a common junction. Sometimes it's because the problem is too embarrassing or too obvious; would puncture a dream or was too personal. If the pioneer found out anything early on, it was that whistles in the dark didn't really keep the wolves at bay.

After accepting the fact that the cavalry ain't comin', and before we start putting our strategy into place, we need to examine three obstacles to success that are becoming increasingly critical to 20th century business.

1. ILLITERACY

It's hard to say it, isn't it? While we proudly introduce our communications systems for Frontier Year 2000, that is, to unite us in total technological networking, we hear a snicker along with a groan.

Today with barely more than a decade remaining in the twentieth century, *27 million Americans are functional illiterates*. One out of five of us, more than the entire population of Canada, can't read and write functionally.

Pick up your favorite business magazine and read the table of contents. Exciting, though it is, with article after article to bring your company to the state of the art, the sobering fact remains that too few employees are capable of comprehending the printed word. When is the last time the first page pictured the editorial board meeting with educators to figure how to teach employees to read and write?

These employees may be able to write their name or trace it or mark a fashionable "X," but they get lost because they can't read the street signs, at least not while they are moving at any speed. They're limited in calling for help because they can't use a telephone directory. They fear the doctor's prescription because they've forgotten how he said to take the pills and they can't read the directions on the bottle. They are suspicious and uptight when buying groceries because they can't count change.

These are the people who will operate your latest million-dollar machinery as you modernize for world competition! Do you recall that mother who almost burned out her child's stomach because she thought the liquid soap was antacid; or what about that farm hand who may come to your employment office desperately needing work because he just about destroyed his herd when he mistook poison for feed?

While the insulated executive rants and raves that the capital expenditures aren't paying off, the *leader* faces what we only whisper in dark corners: of all the nations in the Western world, the United States has one of the highest illiteracy rates. In fact, taking all 158 nations that are members of the United Nations, the United States ranks forty-ninth in illiteracy.

We in the rich nations have increased real gross product in each of twenty decades since James Watt invented the steam engine in the 1780s. Our computers can test in one day more mathematical correlations than Albert Einstein could test in his lifetime. But Russia today has a larger proportion of doctors, scientists, and engineers in their nonagricultural work force than we do.

Today's executive quickly blames the public school system. He ducks responsibility for our illiteracy, fortified with statistics from the latest education crisis reports. He even threatens to sue the local school boards for not delivering the goods.

How serious is the problem? Well, when you hear a member of Congress join with the business community in an effort to balance the budget declaring, "We can't measure the personal cost of inadequate education but we do know the social cost impacts us by *$225 billion annually*," you know it's monumental. Fifty percent of all prison inmates are illiterate. We cannot afford the cost of this human and economic tragedy.

The problem is not new but it has taken on crisis proportions as we've moved forward with technology. And it isn't that we haven't been a literate nation. Our pilgrims organized schools second only to building their churches. In fact, the church buildings were multi-use. They took Psalm 119:105, "Your word is a lamp to my feet and a light to my path," as a cue that education was an expression of their spiritual dedication. When our pioneers settled the West sacrifices were many, including tapping meager resources to build one-room schools.

We're not an emerging nation. We have emerged! But now we've become educational backsliders. Compare the respect an elementary teacher had in your childhood to the respect teachers have today. It isn't that we haven't spent enough dollars. What a contradiction! To the degree we have appreciated the school facilities, we have depreciated the school faculty.

Meeting the Challenges of Illiteracy

Our crisis was brought home to me, not by reading the best sellers of the Peterses, Blanchards, Levensons, Bennises, Reisses, Sheehys, Naisbitts, Garfields. I have enjoyed each, but apparently they considered basic education too mundane to address and not "the stuff" that makes for best sellers. No, I was confronted with the problem during an annual three-lecture appearance at the Southern Industrial Relations Conference. Each year I get to sit in a seminar led by one of my gurus, Dr. George C. Heaton. This youthful man in his seventies lectures not from the perspective of the classroom, but from fifty years of counseling employees on the job.

George Heaton had quality circles in plants while Japan was still cleaning up from the A-bomb. He was teaching bottom-up management while "The Organizational Man" was still being written. He was not ahead of his day, but decades before his time. His strenuous work week is still a minimum of four and a half sixteen-hour days. His client base includes TFI, Dundee Mills, Sara Lee Corporation, Drexel-Heritage, Eastern Air Lines, Champion International, and others. The topic of his lecture for 1986 was "A Year of Great Expectations." Dr. Heaton started by identifying what he considered to be the one negative that could undermine all industrial hope—*illiteracy*. He went on to say: "As we modernize to be competitive in an industry as mature as textiles, we will be denied our competitive edge if we can't find the literate work force. Capital expenditure becomes a study in futility because we can't function efficiently with an unskilled, stagnant work force."

I agree that economic growth depends on the advance of knowledge, but the issue is, do we have a system to make this knowledge productive? Demographically we know our people by work, class, and sex, but what about functional education?

What are we to do?

First, the leader must accept illiteracy as the destructive problem that it is. We'd like to hide it. We don't want to be reminded that Japan has almost 100 percent literacy and graduates 90 percent of its students.

Second, the leader should have his company join in partnership with local educational institutions to correct the problem.

One of the most progressive steps of our era has been the community college movement. In my city of High Point, I serve on the corporate board of Myrtle Desk Company. President Harry Adams joined early with Guilford Technical College to provide high school equivalency classes for employees at company expense. The fact that Myrtle produces the finest manufactured wood desks could be related to this interest by the CEO.

When I pastored in Rock Hill, South Carolina, there was no community college serving the area, so I arranged for classes to be held in our church, even adding a Dale Carnegie course to the curriculum to foster better self-expression.

Today, the world's largest voluntary organization, Laubach, will have over fifty thousand volunteers tutoring adults. Also, I commend IBM for generously pioneering the use of computers for adult education.

Third, the leader must help his employees by taking an interest in their literary education. Any company can easily justify contributions to the local foundation that allows schools to have courses and activities that their minimal school budgets can't accommodate. Also, it is possible to supplement some of your retirees' income by hiring them to teach remedial reading in the schools. Lee Reeder, a brilliant attorney of Kansas City who is long past retirement age, has found renewed vigor through the hours he spends teaching kids to read.

Some years ago when I did more youth counseling, I faced as disruptive a fellow as I had confronted. If you had asked me at the time, I would have considered him incorrigible. After trying my "whole bag of tricks," I accidentally stumbled on the fact that his reading level was at the fifth grade. He could not read adult material. His rebellion was a cover-up for his sense of inferiority. Today he is a useful, well-employed adult, and the turning point was his becoming fully literate.

Up to now, we have been quiet about this problem, but as Dr. Heaton let me know, this problem is screaming for the leader's attention.

2. INFORMATION

Erudite Dr. Chris Hegarty has built a lecture on the topic "How to Stay Informed in Our Overinformed Age." Now that's scratching where we itch, isn't it? We are tired of reading statistical reviews telling us that whereas we had five thousand desk top computers in 1978, we now have 8 million; and someone projected we could have 80 million by 1990. What a ghastly reminder that we may have miscalculated: wherein knowledge is power, information is not necessarily so. I feel that we may be victims of information hucksters.

The term *information age* can cover a wide range of human activity, but essentially it is defined by our use. We can think of micro-chips, gene splicing, robotic productivity, computer networking, and so on. But the information age should mean material or data brought together for a useful purpose. On the one hand the term applies to setting gear chains and electric circuitry guiding a robot while on the other hand it could apply to methodology, software, and systems.

Artificial intelligence, the new revolution of the information society, has more promise than performance. It is built on the idea that there are common denominators for human beings. Artificial intelligence is the invisible hand moving all of us on cue.

Wishful thinking has always led humans to feel somehow independent while locked in regimentation. We want the predictable. Artificial knowledge can review, organize, eliminate our information.

In other words, it can marshal and manage information, but we must not allow it to become a system that manipulates the facts. We must have moral brakes to control our technological horsepower.

Artificial intelligence can't accommodate the unusual or the unexpected. Its reasoning powers are inflexible. Artificial intelligence makes us data-bound while the marketplace cries for intuitive leaders whose creative judgment can cut through endless analysis.

Artificial intelligence can provide us with consistency and costs, but the leader's ingenuity determines the bottom line. Artificial intelligence can place in concrete the culture of the company, but only the leader can express mercy, understanding, forgiveness, hope, and love. As God chose not to send seraphims to deliver His personal message but to have the Word become flesh, the word to us is that artificial intelligence is only effective when used by authentic leaders.

Fred Luconi, CEO of Allied Expert Systems, Inc., relates: "I had barely uttered the phrase 'artificial intelligence' when the executive held up his hand, stopped me in midsentence, and said, 'Look, the last thing I need around here is artificial intelligence. My staff is loaded with the stuff. What I need is real intelligence. Get me some of that, and you've got a sale.' "

Putting the Computer in Its Place

What, then, is the advantage of the information society? The Conference Board asked its CEO members: "What do you think? Do you think the information-technological society is going to have a dramatic effect, a moderate effect, almost no effect?" Alex Pollack concluded that it would have no effect except that CEOs would be expected to do their jobs better.

From a study done by Kepner-Tregoe, Inc. of 821 CEOs and COOs from *Fortune's 500* we know that CEOs do not generally have computer terminals in their offices. Only 27 percent use a computer occasionally, and 50 percent never do. Yet more than 64 percent believe computers may "help my managers do their jobs better."

CEOs do indicate a desire for computer summaries to be used basically in financial analysis and information processing. They concede some computer use in planning and to a lesser degree in telecommunications, scheduling, market trends, margin ratios, and "what if" scenarios. By far the greatest threat they see in computer use is the tendency to bog their managers down with unnecessary data and the substitution of data processing for thinking. Lesser threats mentioned are high costs, security problems, inaccurate data, digression from work assignments, and poor management of the computer itself.

The Kepner-Tregoe study asked the executives if computers helped them do their jobs better. Their response was, "No. They are tools for people who do tasks—not managers. Executives are paid too much to develop computer skills. Executives are being paid to analyze and implement."

Other CEOs cautioned against the dehumanization of decision making. Computers take judgment out of decisions. They lead to loss of personal touch with raw data and a loss of hands-on experience with facts. One executive warned against "becoming too data-bound." There will always be a place for intuitive and creative judgment which can cut through endless analysis. The CEOs would definitely question *Time* magazine's judgment in naming the computer "Man of the Year" in 1982.

So it falls to the lot of people like Allan Hurst, a quasi-adjunct professor at the University of Michigan, to help future leaders to focus properly. Although CEOs don't use computers, some still have an unfortunate tendency to see them as a potential cavalry.

At a meeting of Furman University's Advisory Board, I entered into a lengthy argument with a fellow member, a rather prominent CEO, who was beseeching this basically undergraduate institution to produce graduates that could, the next day, impact his EDP or MIS or AI. My reply was that a college should not be a trade school limited to teaching skills for twenty-first-century tools, but an institution that could also impart an understanding of the culture of our day.

Naturally I was refreshed to see the unique balance the Furman faculty later designed. The students use the computer for efficiency to learn about the liberal arts.

Furman thinks the computer has only three purposes in assisting the corporate leader:

1. To see fully
2. To think clearly
3. To act wisely.

Furman should receive a hardy "way to go" from business leaders, for they couldn't establish a better plan for being informed in an overinformed society. Let's examine the Furman Plan:

1. To See Fully. Away with the cartoons of the computer expert whose home is dominated by a screen or the marriage counselor asked by the husband to help break up the affair between his wife and her PC.

It took Johannes Kepler, the seventeenth-century astronomer, four years to calculate the orbit of Mars. Today a computer can do it in seconds. Reaction time has been so reduced in our lifetime that we now turn to information technology to give us a rapid infrastructure.

Ross Perot, when asked why GM needed his company, replied that GM did not have four years to develop a new model and become competitive.

Whenever I wonder why we have to see fully and quickly, I think about the cowboy's horse. The horse was domesticated about 2500 B.C. but the stirrup, which is very helpful in riding the horse and absolutely essential if you are going to wage war from that horse, was not developed until 500 A.D. In 1776 it took George Washington three days to go from Boston to New York. It would have taken Alexander the Great the same three days, hundreds of years before.

So to say that each generation has had the same amount of change is not true.

Today, we turn to the computer to give us quick information. Somehow I associate the use of information technology to what I learned as a catcher; that is, keeping the ball squarely in front of me. The computer, with its fast read, keeps the action in front of us so we can see fully.

2. *To Think Clearly.* Although we talk about "the loneliness of leadership"—and nothing can eradicate that —it helps to have the benefit of as much collective human thinking as possible. Unfortunately, time pressures seldom allow us to go around the boardroom. The computer does give us rapid networking or computer conferencing. The American Productivity Center has developed EIES (Electronic Information Exchange System). This system introduced by Jack Grayson compensates for the deficient typing skills of most top-level executives.

In Lakeland, Florida, I found another example. Publix Markets, where President Mark Hollis continues to fan the flame of excellence ignited by George Jenkins, felt a need for faster information input. Publix operates with four key profit and loss centers: grocery, meat, deli, and bakery operations. For years they had used the same P&L format; it was accurate but incomplete and slow.

Publix encourages family involvement. Mark Hollis, himself the second generation in the food business, is now flanked by two sons, Clayton and Jack. Both are equally devoted to people. Clayton, outgoing, never meets a stranger and is ideal for public interaction. Jack, shy and reflective, has computer skills, and asked the department managers what type of P&L would give them faster and clearer daily control.

After letting them virtually serve as designers, Jack developed the model that uniquely reflects their need and assists Mark in his decision making.

3. *To Act Wisely.* Whether the information support is viable or not comes right down to the quality of the action taken.

More information than necessary might be the exception rather than the rule. Leadership disciplines itself by prioritizing the information to gain full visibility of the problem, clear thinking, and wise action.

Our food industry had difficulty in disciplining itself with the information available from the scanner. Up front we gave the wrong signal to the public —that the scanner was installed so that they could be moved through the checkout faster and, hopefully, more accurately. Then we found the public wasn't in such a rush. But we did discover that the greater value of the scanner was the control we gained of our store. We learned what people want and don't want when we have more product than shelves. We learned which product produces the most profit, the pace of product turnover, and costs of productivity.

There is a flip side. A body of information can just lie there and mold unless it is acted upon. Union Carbide in India, the Chernobyl meltdown in Russia, and the loss of our seven astronauts in the *Challenger* explosion, were, it seems to me, the result of information ignored.

Information always sounds appetizing. But value only results when information is moved from romance to reality, from unrelated fact to balanced action.

3. INTEGRATION

Some of the Western adventurers limped into Fort Laramie. Many never made it. In the early weeks, the attrition rate was shocking. So the fort served as a happy meeting place where unrelated and even competing adventurers could band together for common survival.

Our new frontier demands the same.

The enterprise system of today is fueled by competition, and enlightened competitors know common meeting ground is above the daily fray. World competition has reduced the adversarial relationship among business leaders.

Commonly, we hear that our progress is impeded by the breakdown between business and government. "We just don't have enough business people in government," is the complaint. But doesn't a government reflect its people, especially in an openly elected government? When the businesses fight among themselves, doesn't it stand to reason that it's easy to dig a trench between the private and public sectors?

We are approaching the threshold of the third century of our constitutional government. We come to this milestone with some remarkably favorable conditions. We have enjoyed four decades of peace in Europe, which has never occurred before, and the Pacific is tranquil. Management and labor quarrel, but bloody strikes are not known to my children. The cancer of inflation is in remission. Our quality of life bespeaks our discretionary income. No longer the domain of a few "health nuts," physical fitness has moved to general acceptance. We have wept over our blunders in Vietnam and restored the beauty of our flag.

In one sentence: there is not a problem that we have imposed on our system that we, the people, can't correct within it.

The majority of contemporary books stress how to manage others, how to get others to be productive. Few dare write about managing oneself and expect the book to be read. Yet, development is self-development.

From my own father's land of Lebanon comes the picture of leadership, the shepherd, who was a local hero. He cared for his flock as though they were human. He made the sheep familiar with his voice before he moved them out. That's why Jesus said, "I am the good shepherd . . . I know my sheep. . . . and they will hear My voice. . . ."

The herding of sheep in Wyoming would be totally foreign to the shepherd of the Near East. When my own grandfather moved the sheep, he led them, chanting their names as he walked. When the sheep followed, there was nowhere they went but that his footprint was already there. When the sheep sensed danger or, as David wrote in Psalm 23, "walk[ed] through the valley of the shadow of death," my grandfather would simply walk through the flock lifting each one's ear and whispering its name to it. That leadership receives well-deserved trust.

How does the leader keep himself worthy of his role? Who talks to the CEO? With the money we pour into training of subordinates, does that mean the leader has arrived and doesn't need such? No, it must be done on a peer level and above the competitive battles of the companies being led. Today's frontier demands a camaraderie among leaders of comparable responsibility. This need should be met by the professional association.

Hopefully, I don't sound too biased, but after addressing the major business and professional associations of this country, I can find no better example of what I'm talking about than the Food Marketing Institute, which brings together all elements of the wholesale and retail food business. It is just now dawning on America that the combined weight and ubiquitousness of the food industry make it the largest in our country. We may not live by bread alone, but we cannot live without bread either.

The president of FMI is Robert O. Aders. He is the ideal fit: a lawyer with service as CEO of Kroger Company and undersecretary of labor. His astute mind does not indulge fuzzy thinking.

Bob felt that in order to have the confidence of the public, the food industry had to have a singular purpose, so FMI has adopted the motto "The purchasing agent for the consumer," which means the association will work diligently to guard against disarray in the marketplace, either by production or agricultural crisis that would affect the prices at the kitchen table or the lunch counter.

The unique facet of FMI is not its multidimensional training programs or its research arm of government relations, but its ability to challenge the CEOs of the industry to keep their common interests above competitive or colloquial problems.

How is this accomplished? Bob and the corps of elected officers meticulously plan the board meetings and the interchange conferences with National American Wholesale Grocers Association (NAWGA) and Grocery Manufacturers Association (GMA). The focal point, however, is the midyear meeting of CEOs. Taking a phrase from the turn of the century, FMI Mid-Year Conference provides program content "to afflict the comfortable and comfort the afflicted." Bob Aders sees to it that none of us become complacent or stale. The perks and protection of a corporate office tend to leave one spiritually starved, physically bloated, and intellectually fatigued. This condition diminishes the inventiveness and the restless courage needed to address the problems in our new climate. Leaders meet with their peers to restore freshness.

The action side of FMI is in government relations. For while we bemoan the adversarial relationship between business and government, we also have an enviable record of government and the private sector working together. Our World War II victory was the proof of a united nation. But the unity didn't begin there or stop there. While government resented a Charlie Wilson saying from his seat as CEO of GM, "What's good for GM is good for America," business also rejects illogical Congressional regulations that disrupt our competitive edge.

"Divide and conquer" has worked for government ever since Julius Caesar initiated the strategy. Through professional associations we have the opportunity to speak with a unified voice.

We can't have it both ways for sure. We can't expect government to cover our business failures. When Jack Crocker was leading the rocket growth of Super Valu, he kept reminding his staff that they could not expect any artificial protection. He was in concert with Dr. Rhodes Boyson, a member of Britain's Parliament and a respected author who wrote: "Trying to have a free enterprise system without bankruptcy is like trying to have Christianity without hell."

So we know the role of government is not to protect our business from merciless competition. All we ask is that our government not put such a heavy foot on our business as to tilt the playing field for the competition. We know there must be strenuous effort on our part for the development, manufacture, sale, and service of our products along with constant reinvestment in modern methods of technology. We just resent government's taking action on exaggerated earnings.

Is it wrong for us to expect government to provide a climate conducive to the life and growth of vigorous efforts? We know the ultimate judge as to whether our business is more deserving than the competition is not whether government worked for us, but whether we have worked smartly enough with the labor and capital available to attract the consumer to our product or service.

Actually, the tension between government and business is not new. From Teddy Roosevelt and his "trust busters" to John Kennedy's glaring denunciation employing "four-letter words," our love/hate relationship has waxed and waned.

When business enjoyed a robust growth, we felt we could afford government intrusion, and government, for its part, gleefully gathered its taxes and mushroomed the bureaucratic head count. Neither one needed the other. With our new economic realities, we realize that government and business can no longer afford the luxury of being adversaries if our nation is to be competitive.

Business must produce quality products competitively priced and cannot afford the weight of government barnacles. Robert Fegley of General Electric comments:

> The world economy has become highly politicized. Costs are inflated, expenditures are mandated, inefficiencies are imposed; markets are created and destroyed by decisions made in the presidiums and legislatures of the world.
>
> If the business manager fails to learn how to anticipate and influence these public policy decisions, he is going to find his life full of unpleasant and unmanageable surprises.

In my association with business leaders I find they want neither a bailout nor a Band-Aid. They aren't lobbying for restrictive trade nor grants for research and development. Neither is dollar manipulation or unfair tax advantage on their agenda. They are only asking to be left unencumbered of weighty, unnecessary regulations so they can get off the starting blocks fairly.

Unfortunately, too many executives who don't become leaders think that citing the problem of government intervention ends their role. After all, they're "busy, busy, busy." True leaders unite their efforts in organizations like FMI and work on the problems. The tax restructuring was led by corporate leaders like John Bryan, who knew that the immediate effect would cost his business, but that in the long term it was right for the country. Byron Allumbaugh, CEO of Ralph's, competes in the toughest retail food market of our nation. Yet he shuttled back and forth to Washington, D.C., as often as FMI called for his help. Upon completing his term as FMI chairman, he accepted the leadership of the California Retailers Association. In reply to my letter of congratulations and appreciation, he stated: "The CRA is our most effective state lobbying association in Sacramento. As you know, a lot of crazy legislation is introduced in California; and if we don't stop it here, it seems to quickly roll across the country."

Contrast this with my bewilderment a few years back when I discovered that the son of the founder of one of America's great world companies felt he and his team should not be active in politics for their sole responsibility was to manufacture successfully, no matter what party won or who occupied the White House or which person served as governor of New York where they had corporate headquarters.

The late George Meany and I usually found ourselves on opposite sides of political arguments, but I always admired him because I knew where he stood, what he believed, and what he wanted. He used his political muscle to raise millions of dollars for the candidates of his choice. Instead of criticizing him, I call upon leaders to emulate him.

Candidates are front persons for the vested interests that have tapped them to be spokespersons. So it is logical that before you endorse a person, even a buddy or former classmate, find out who his intimates are, his kitchen cabinet, his close advisors. As laborious as it is, read the candidate's speeches, books, and articles. Face the candidate in a frank discussion, and ask him to respond in a memo. Candidates do tend to have "writer's cramp" on sensitive issues.

No, I'm not saying "buy a candidate," but help elect someone who expresses your views. And after the election stay close to your representative. As the late Eugene Talmadge said, "We politicians have become so bad that we won't even stay bought."

So I'm using the word *integration*, not in a racial sense but in a comparative one. Strong leaders whose companies compete head-on must join in common interests and action. Your professional association must become the catalyst to challenge your continued growth and to dialogue with our government.

At the fort, the adventurers who had smugly started out from St. Louis laughed at how naive they really had been. Much wiser now, they had a better grip on what to expect. The frontier still loomed as a Promised Land, but promised lands always exact a high price. True leaders find the adventure worth the price.

5

Loadin' the Wagons

When the wagon master first met his westward bound "pilgrims," it was always with a mixture of laughter and frustration—laughter because of the total ignorance of most about the absolute necessities for the four-month journey; frustration because of the pilgrims' insistence on bringing all of their earthly possessions with them. When taxed with excess weight, the oxen pulling the wagon could not ford streams and climb mountains. When one views those Conestoga wagons today in Western museums, the small dimensions are startling.

The wagon master knew the limitations of the equipment and worked within them. He knew the unbridled optimism of his wagon families would soon enough be bridled by the elements. His goal was not to have them giddy at the beginning of the trip and weeping at the end, but earnest at the start and brimming with excitement as they arrived at the Willamette Valley in Oregon or Sutter's Fort in California.

A successful ending was set in motion by a disciplined beginning. The wagon train averaged from ten to fifteen miles a day on the two-thousand mile trip. They had to be sure to cross the Sierra Nevadas or the Cascades before the first snowflakes fell or they would be trapped in the monumental snows through the winter when they were at their lowest physical and psychological ebb. A wagon master's miscalculation of timing and load factors could cause a repetition of the Donner party tragedy, an appalling chronicle of pioneers who, caught in the winter snows, fell to cannibalism to survive all because the wagon master waited too late in May to holler "Westward Ho."

It was a matter of timing. The pioneers left Missouri early in May, but not too early because they wanted to roll across the plains by June so their oxen and horses would find lush grass. If on schedule, they would carve their names on Independence Rock by July 4 and note that one-third of the trip was behind them.

Whereas the adventurers did most of their thinking and planning in the saddle, the wagon masters planned ahead for emergencies, depending not just on their knowledge, but on their ability to lead.

The Joy of Decision Making

Decisions that affect us are serious enough but when our decisions affect others, that seriousness is compounded.

Our reluctance, and even fear, about decision making, I feel, is due to more than just our conscientiousness. It is almost folklore that decisions should be hard to make. And if they are not, then we are labeled calloused and uncaring.

I made my first difficult decision in my school days. I was at least four weeks into my first year of high school Latin before I realized I liked Latin and could do it. At first I was reluctant to admit my love, lest I be considered odd. Then I was bombarded with warnings and taunts. I remember only one positive comment: "Latin is the easiest and surest way to understand English."

I liked Latin all three years and had little difficulty knocking down an *A*. I hid my pleasure from my classmates. The rumors of many school years had already sealed their verdict: Latin is to be dreaded! But my study of Latin led to an offer from Colgate for a full scholarship. (Colgate had found that Latin teachers were in great demand.)

A few years later, when I had to make some substantial decisions, I heard again the discouraging words of my Latin days. Again, a mountain was being made out of a molehill. It took awhile to realize that decision making was natural, and I had been making them by instinct even before I knew the word *decision*. Hunger made me decide whether or not to swallow mother's milk. Circumstances and results determined my decision to obey my parents. Life was connected by linked decisions, and at an early age I realized I could be a forger of links.

Calling decisions "natural events" doesn't mean decisions are easy. We improve our decision-making ability only by making decisions. However, we are caught on the horns of a dilemma. On the one side, the post-counter-culture generations specialize in putting off decisions, even on routine matters. Should I marry? Why have children now? Should I change my career path without a new opportunity, or should I stay bored? Members of the counter-culture tend to hide behind what they consider a democratic approach to leadership. The very word *leadership* defies democracy. The wagon train would never have crossed the wide Missouri if it had depended on consensus or committee.

On the other hand, we describe our leaders in extremely aggressive "macho" terms: "barn-burner," "trash-mover," "shaker and a mover," "Trojan." It is as though we base decision making upon tape measuring the biceps.

One of the first revelations I discovered in corporate circles amazed me:

I noted how laid back, gentle, and genteel were those leaders getting the best results. They were devoid of bluster and blow; their leadership showed substance and sense.

Not every gentle person is a decision maker, but a decisive person usually promotes gentleness. In fact, often business irritations, preoccupation, stresses, and short-temperedness toward staff associates fester because the executive is unable or unwilling to make a decision.

Silent, like a ship gliding through deep waters, are the gentle people who lead our corporations, often in operations that reach around the world. The more decisive they are, the kinder they are. You find such leaders not vehement nor violent, for they have neither paranoia nor insecurity. Long ago they matured beyond the point of "the louder I shout, the less certain I am." Their voices are calm; their words are rational; their actions are measured. The rush, the panic, the pushing, the irritability that come from indecisions or an ill-defined decision is missing.

"He who reigns within himself, and rules passions, desires and fears, is more than a king," wrote John Milton centuries ago. The statement could well describe John Burnside Smith, as I've watched him for twenty-five years heading the Mayflower Corporation. His charismatic father, John Sloan Smith, if he were living today, would walk into my office and, I'm sure, before he left, I would have signed in as a Mayflower franchisee.

Upon John Sloan's sudden death, John B. stepped into his father's shoes. Here is this rather big, but quiet although gregarious, self-effacing John B. who is inheriting one of the most recognized names in the industry, though it was still a one-dimensional company that knew difficult decisions had to be made. Even though each of his father's senior advisors opposed his moves, he, with his quiet tenacity, kept moving forward, taking the stock public while watching the value increase 250 percent on the American Stock Exchange, fighting off a corporate raider, designing an LBO. John B. has shown his recognition that life is primarily links connected by decisions.

Boston's famous Lahey Clinic found that the inability or slowness to make decisions can cause chronic fatigue, which can lead to physical disorder. Indecision, they found, played a major role in psychic disorders. We can accept fatigue related to "a running cold, virus, or chemical imbalance," but we are dismayed when we are physically sound but emotionally whipped. A day of strenuous labor followed by accomplishment and satisfaction leads to contented sleep and a zest for the next day of opportunities. Fatigue caused by indecision results in agonizing nights of tossing and turning, and we awake more tired than when we retired.

As Bertrand Russell remarks, it is amazing how much happiness and efficiency can be increased by the cultivation of an orderly mind, which thinks about a matter at the right time rather than inadequately at other times. When a difficult or worrying decision has to be reached, as soon as all the data is available, give the matter your best thought and make your decision; having made the decision, do not revise it unless some new fact comes to your knowledge. Nothing is so exhausting as indecision and nothing so futile.

The Zenon Hansen Style of Decison Making

Zenon C. R. Hansen has made decision making an art form. In his forty-three years as a trucking industry leader, his companies never suffered a strike. To the casual observer he may look burly and blustery, but we who know him know the gentleness underneath. He makes the tough decisions in sales or in labor comfortably and rapidly. His decisiveness brought comfort and confidence to his employees and led to unusually high executive productivity.

Was Zenon's decision making a natural gift that some have and others don't? No, I don't think so, but circumstances play a part. Although he had caring guardians, Zenon was literally on his own from the age of ten. No child labor laws protected him. As a teenager he was working in Florida from 7:00 A.M. to 11:00 P.M. on non-school days. He did not regret having to work, but cherished the opportunity.

At age nineteen he went to France where his response to circumstances helped his decision making. He formed an impression not of the world's bigness, but of its smallness and the universal similarity of people's needs and wants. During those years in Europe he sharpened his manners, nurturing his natural respect for people. He felt that as a free citizen of the United States, he had an inheritance even greater than that of the wealthy and powerful of Paris.

Living in an adult world at the end of his teen-age years, Zenon learned that life has compensating balances: men, regardless of their titles, started each day by putting on their pants the same way. He was just as capable as the next person. This wasn't cockiness; it was accepting his capabilities. Also, on his own, he realized that only he could make decisions for himself. His survival could well depend on his decisiveness. It was not surprising to me to see that, in later life, his circle of friends included General Douglas MacArthur, Biggie Munn, and Vince Lombardi.

Zenon has always felt:

It is better to make a decision than be caught and hit in the middle of an intersection by taking too long to decide whether to turn left or right.

The Bible supports this idea (Revelation 3). When the Apostle John wrote to the seven churches in Asia Minor, he singled out the church at Laodicea, reporting that God was not chastening that church for any misdeeds but for being indecisive. "You are neither hot nor cold," John wrote, and went on to say that because the church was lukewarm, God would like to literally "spew you out of My mouth."

Zenon Hansen understood well that decision making was not an option but an obligation of the leader. Decision making is not an object of dread but a door to enlarged opportunity. The proof? When Zenon retired, Mack was the world leader in its class of trucks. When he took over as CEO, Wall Street predicted the demise of the fine old truck manufacturer. Zenon soon made the firm number one in its class in the world.

■I■I■I■I■I■I■I■I■I■I■I■I■I■I■I■I■I■I■I■I■I■I■I■I■I■I■I■I■I■I■I■I■I■I■I■I■I■I■I■I■

Now, I wish I could give you a foolproof formula for decision making. Since it is the extension of a leader's personality, there are not two people who decide alike. We know that nothing can energize a company more quickly than the leader making a courageous decision or rally a company more quickly than the leader making a tough decision. A decision should not be made out of fear, nor can a leader ever fear making a decision. Leaders make decisions smoothly and with relative ease, yet not carelessly. More than anything else, the landslide victory of President Reagan was based on the public's feeling that Reagan could face issues without hysteria and calmly resolve them. Americans were ready for the return of Eisenhower's soothing style.

No one can give a step-by-step formula. In my studies,

however, I find certain common ingredients. A crisis decision doesn't allow a leader time to go through a procedural countdown. But instinctively or not, leaders do follow the sequence outlined.

I. ANALYZE

Analysis before action. One of the buzz expressions today is that successful companies command their executives by shouting: "Ready, fire, aim." That's ridiculous! It may happen in an emergency as a last resort, but successful companies do not leap before they look. The phrase isn't new because writers thirty years ago were writing about companies leaping before looking. Remember, Prime Minister Lloyd George of England warned, "It's hazardous to leap a chasm in two jumps."

Ed Walzer, the philosophic and witty editor-in-chief of *Progressive Grocer*, adds a new twist to some old generalizations:

> 1. Competition influences decision making. Ed's comment: "The trouble with joining the rat race is that, even if you win, you're still a rat." Or, "The lion may lay down with the lamb but the lamb won't get much sleep." Or, "Though your competition beats their swords into plowshares, they may bury you in the plowing."
>
> 2. When it comes to forward planning and decision making, Ed feels an old aphorism still applies: "Assumption is the mother of all screw-ups."
>
> 3. Leadership is necessary in decision making. Ed comments: "The secret of executive success is sincerity. . . once you fake that, you've got it made."

The analysis process may sound trite, but my observation of corporations indicates that the failure to analyze is instrumental in the sabotage of most decisions. Now I mean real analysis—not sitting around and getting sidetracked by such buzz words as: *orchestrate, optimize, quantitize, implement, interface, linear programming,* and *econometric planning.*

Dr. J. Finley Lee, distinguished professor of business administration at the University of North Carolina, cautions us to begin our analysis by asking obvious, but essential, questions. Addressing the Montgomery Mutual Insurance Company, Dr. Lee advised them that they begin with these three basic questions:

1. What are you going to sell and when?
2. What should your objectives be in the case of priorities, performance, and results?
3. What decisions will I need to make to achieve these results, by way of managing myself and my company?

Herbert E. Hawkes wrote:

"Half the worry in the world is caused by people trying to make decisions before they have sufficient knowledge."

Royal Dutch Shell, in their criteria for selecting promising executives, whom they call "Crown Princes," seeks the analytic ability in their applicants. Then, they couple analytic ability with a "helicopter"quality, that is, the ability to see the whole picture. Their criteria suggest seeing from a hovering, low-flying helicopter, not a distant, fast *Concorde*. They're looking for an ability high enough to see the full picture but low enough to note essential details.

Our analytic ability is aided in this computer age as long as we maintain a balance between the statistical data from the computer and our intuitive feelings.

Analysis doesn't mean instant decision but rather planned performance. Downing Jenks took over the troubled Missouri-Pacific Railroad in the late 1950s. Although quick action was needed, he spent his first days studying what he had and—even more—what he didn't. Working with Downing in our mutual hobby, the Boy Scouts of America, I learned that better than anyone else, he knew what he didn't know. He often caught colleagues off guard as they were expecting to be sold or lobbied by saying, "Fellows, I don't have the foggiest notion what we should do. What do you suggest?" This approach caught Allegheny Corporation by surprise and led to the strategy that, after years of struggle, enabled the railroad to be reorganized, recapitalized, and *free*.

The difference between Downing and some of us is that he

doesn't stop the analysis process when he feels he has enough data for the immediate problem. He lets the analysis run its full course. So when Missouri-Pacific took off and had many of us rushing to buy stock; when the railroad was becoming the sixth in size; when we were admiring his customized customer service that listened; when he developed automatic freight houses allowing the railroad to profitably advertise handling "Less than a truckload; Less than a carload"; when he arranged fair interchange with Mexico, Downing was talking of *merger*.

Merger plans when he had everything going his way? Downing had the advantage not only of current analysis, but as a third generation "railroader," he was also demonstrating that nothing is more valuable than experience. Having historic perspective and current efficiency, he could talk merger, not absorption. M-P would bring continuing profits to the bottom line. So twenty years after first feeling merger was the future, Downing folded his M-P into Union Pacific, which one analyst said was like "merging the Dallas Cowboys with the Pittsburgh Steelers."

Analysis is identifying the need for a decision followed by where and when you want to arrive.

II. FANTASIZE

Do you imagine things visually, in pictures? If so, fantasizing is natural for you.

Some years ago while under contract with GM, I addressed an Oldsmobile leadership team in Lansing, Michigan, and we did just that: we fantasized. I gave them a problem and then asked them to draw a picture of their response to the problem from the perspective of their area of responsibility. Now their artwork would have flunked the first grade, for the majority of them hadn't been to the drawing board since their last coloring book, but the result in the identification of their response was *magna cum laude*.

We cannot be Einsteins, but there is this poignant point in his diary: "When I have examined myself and my methods of thought, I come to the conclusion that the gift of *fantasy* has meant more to me than *my talent for absorbing positive knowledge*" (emphasis added).

We have been gifted with the ability to daydream, to relive the past as well as walk into the future through the eye of fantasy. Daydreaming in our childhood may have been used as an escape from the unpleasant, but it was also our way of reaching with hope into the future. Interestingly, studies show that when children start the regimen of school, it inhibits their daydreaming. So, I guess I'm suggesting we really reach back to our youth to loosen our fantasizing.

There is not a conflict between the pragmatist and the dreamer in leadership. They are complementary. The doing is the extension of the dreaming.

Creative solitude has its own reward. It increases one's confidence and capacity to achieve objectives. Solitude helps us face frustrations and uncertainties and fantasize them into proper sequence. President Woodrow Wilson felt that "All big men are dreamers. They see things in the soft haze of a spring day or the red fire of a long winter's evening. Some of us let these dreams die but others nourish and protect them, nurse them through bad days until they bring them to the sunshine and light which comes always to those who sincerely hope that their dreams will come true." Robert Browning wrote: "Trust is within ourselves, it takes no rise from outward things, whate'er you may believe . . . and to know rather consists in opening out a way whence the imprisoned splendor may escape, then in effecting entry for a light supposed to be without."

Some of us tend to enjoy activity more than we do our dreaming or fantasizing. We allow the noise and commotion of our routine to drown out our inner selves and our real goals. This fantasizing can be done while strolling down a busy street, walking in the backyard, or shutting off the phone for a few moments in the office.

Ironically, the fantasizing that may start out as nebulous ends up giving us focus.

75

III. VISUALIZE

No, I'm not being redundant when I follow fantasize with visualize. Fantasizing is stretching our minds to the outer limits of our imaginations. The ultimate decision will use both fantasy and fact, mixing these two ingredients into a composite. Now, with the composite in hand, we can visualize the impact of the proposed decision upon all people and elements involved.

The leader is required to be not only visionary and far-sighted but also pragmatic, for he must take the pulse of those who will be involved in and impacted by his decision.

The late N. C. English taught me more about visualizing than anyone else. The most unwelcome person in his office was the fellow rushing in and shouting, "Nee, we've got to make a decision and *you've* got to make it now!" His Quaker raising served him well. He just didn't believe that "the Spirit would move him" until he had a chance to study the effect the move would have on all involved. He believed he should do everything with and through people, and they aren't inspired by impetuous and arbitrary action.

I can still hear his advice to me:

"Tom, when I'm in the dark, I stand still. That way, at least, I won't step into a hole."

To him, profit and loss were secondary to people impact, for long term profit and loss were really in the hands of the people. Although Nee was retiring and somewhat shy with all but his circle of friends, he built Carolina Underwear into a success case study by always thinking in terms of people and visualizing the effect of his decisions upon them.

In his plants worked secure, upbeat employees who knew Nee had high expectations of them but also knew he was reasonable. That feeling brought his firm to market leadership, which is the only real job protection. Nee visualized himself walking in the shoes of his employees whether at work or at the minor league baseball field where he reserved a special section for them.

Decisions are not made in a vacuum.

Rhiny Reinhart of Gateway Foods believes in visualizing. As soon as he develops the analysis picture fully, he seeks to put it on the mind screen of his key executives.

From humble beginnings and few, very few, dollars, Rhiny has built Gateway Foods into the largest wholesale food company owned by one individual. Annual sales are well in excess of $1 billion. Rhiny is a master at leveraging his assets, but he says with a grin, "Never to the extent you can't face your bankers eyeball to eyeball." Rhiny makes me think of the words from the Country and Western band Alabama: "They didn't know nothing about a silver spoon. But they knew about the Golden Rule."

Rhiny wants a growth company; he wants profits; he's restless to be the country's most efficient distributor; but he feels the decisions necessary must first be seen and believed in by the core team. Rhiny has chosen carefully and pays much more than industry average salaries to those who help him sharpen the focus of his decisions.

Rhiny believes totally in the visualizing aspect of decision making, with an added wrinkle:

The only thing better than one person seeing the vision is several people seeing the vision.

IV. MORALIZE

Leaders, even when forced to make a fast decision, have a built-in check and balance system. B. C. Forbes wrote years ago, "Life is not complex. The man of fixed, ingrained principles, who has mapped out a straight course, and has the courage and self-control to adhere to it, does not find life complex. Things are so ordained that, in the end, we reap if we faint not—and deserve to reap, of course. Complexities are all of our own making."

Denying that decisions have a moral dimension can be the first step into the ruthless, dark side of the private enterprise system. The casual reader of Adam Smith thinks all he did was design and promote a free enterprise system. Actually much of his writing and teaching accepted prosperity as a "known," but questioned if we had the character and moral strength to manage our prosperity.

Such danger must have also been in the mind of G. K. Chesterton when he commented, "A paradox of great humility is the matter of sins combined with great ferocity in the matter of ideas."

Herb Taylor was thought to be out of balance. He didn't stop with moralizing; he spiritualized. His friends whispered that he really should go to preaching and leave business to them. They admired him for organizing InterVarsity Christian Fellowship for collegians on secular campuses. Many of their children were helped by Young Life that he started for teenagers. Both organizations went national and international. But a tough businessman making hard decisions? Never. So they stood in amazement as Herb Taylor took bankrupt Club Aluminum and made it a record breaker in the industry. Herb Taylor believed, as do most respected leaders, that there is a relationship between morality and profitability.

Proper employee relations is just another angle to the face of ethics. Every day Herb asked himself four questions that are now known the world over as Rotary International's 4-Way Test:

1. Is it the truth?
2. Is it fair to all concerned?
3. Will it build good will and better friendship?
4. Will it be beneficial to all concerned?

Totally rejecting the idea that the end would justify the means, Herb Taylor believed moral decisions had good endings.

Maybe I am telling too much about myself when I admit that I do, on occasion, watch evening soaps. My friends think the few moments when I escape are spent reading or playing tennis, but I watch *Dallas* and justify the waste of time by reading while I watch. J. R. brought me straight out of my chair during one of the episodes when he was blackmailing a government official. The official, trying to hide his failure from the past, begs J. R. not to blackmail him over it and make him compromise his position. The devilish J. R., of course, can't let him off the hook. Patting the official on the back, he says, "Don't worry—once you've let integrity go, everything else is a piece of cake."

Can you afford to moralize a decision? That's not the question. Can you afford not to moralize a decision?

The Johnson & Johnson Credo and the Tylenol Crisis

Read carefully this statement written at the close of World War II by a young brigadier general anxious to cycle back into the private sector:

> Institutions, both public and private, exist because the people want them, believe in them, or at least are willing to tolerate them. The day is past when business was a private matter, if it ever really was. In a business society, every act of business has social consequences and may arouse public interest. Every time business hires, builds, sells or buys, it is acting for the people, as well as for itself, and it *must* accept full responsibility for its acts.

The writer was Robert Wood Johnson, who was heir to Johnson and Johnson. The statement became the preamble of a corporate document he entitled simply "Our Credo."

Our Credo

We believe our first responsibility
is to the doctors, nurses and patients,
to mothers and all others who use our products and services.
In meeting their needs
everything we do must be of high quality.
We must constantly strive to reduce our costs
in order to maintain reasonable prices.
Customers' orders must be serviced promptly and accurately.
Our suppliers and distributors must have an opportunity
to make a fair profit.

We are responsible to our employees,
the men and women who work with us throughout the world.
Everyone must be considered as an individual.
We must respect their dignity and recognize their merit.
They must have a sense of security in their jobs.
Compensation must be fair and adequate,
and working conditions clean, orderly and safe.
Employees must feel free to make suggestions and complaints.
There must be equal opportunity for employment, development
and advancement for those qualified.
We must provide competent management,
and their actions must be just and ethical.
We are responsible to the communities
in which we live and work
and to the world community as well.
We must be good citizens—support good works and charities
and bear our fair share of taxes.
We must encourage civic improvement
and better health and education.
We must maintain in good order
the property we are privileged to use,
protecting the environment and natural resources.

Our final responsibility is to our stockholders.
Business must make a sound profit.
We must experiment with new ideas.
Research must be carried on, innovative programs developed
and mistakes paid for.
New equipment must be purchased, new facilities provided
and new products launched.
Reserves must be created to provide for adverse times.
When we operate according to these principles,
the stockholders should realize a fair return.

Johnson & Johnson

The validity of the statement was sorely tested on September 29, 1982, and again in 1986 with the Tylenol crises, the poisonous tampering with medicine capsules which caused the deaths of innocent users.

Johnson & Johnson chairman, Jim Burke, must still feel it was yesterday. He was heading a company known for its healthy corporate culture. I don't use "healthy" as a pun. It was a company shaped by "The General" and known for its generous gifts to eleemosynary organizations and educational institutions from the Robert Wood Foundation. Nathan Pusey, President of Harvard, said, "The least that can be expected from a CEO according to 'The General'—Robert Wood Johnson—is to pronounce the name of God without embarrassment." Now Jim Burke and the company were unintentional accessories to the use of their Tylenol capsules in poisoning lives.

When I managed the Boy Scouts of America from the national headquarters in North Brunswick, New Jersey, we were neighbors with J & J and I saw that they deserved our respect.

Jim Burke had started his administration studying whether "Our Credo" really reflected a corporation with well over 100 companies around the world, highly decentralized, each with its own separate mission. Did the credo that had significance in the home office "wash" hundreds of miles away? The study seemingly led individuals to check and revive their own values. After three years of study the managers of all 152 companies assembled in New York in 1979 to express commitment to the revitalized "Our Credo." But that was before Tylenol.

J & J believed from the beginning that they must never offer for sale any product that might prove to be a hazard to a person's health. Beginning September 29, 1982, at the outset of the "Tylenol Crisis," people were dying, families were suffering, threats of lawsuits were running rampant. A CEO, but not a leader, would have panicked, tucked tail, and hid, returning years later with a similar product under a totally different logo. But Jim Burke is a leader. He established a crisis team, encouraged total openness with the press, and expressed deep sympathy for the sufferers.

To bring immediate calm, Burke and his team recalled the product, contrary to the wishes of both the FBI and the FDA who considered the destruction of the product a surrender to blackmail. J & J felt their credibility depended upon the public being assured that they never for a moment equated corporate economic loss with the loss of life.

Paramount in J & J's thinking were two questions: Was J & J involved? If so, who in particular was involved?

When they were comfortable that the tragedy was totally orchestrated outside J & J, then a new obligation faced them. Removal of potential hazard was a corporate obligation. Equally, they were charged to create, provide, and preserve products beneficial to the public. Tylenol was that kind of product, so J & J licked its wounds and returned the product to the shelf. When you are moralizing a decision, it doesn't mean only that you won't do a wrong thing but also that you will fight positively for that which is right. By 1986, Tylenol had recovered its market share of one-third of the pain relief market, despite the early prophecies of doom.

In 1986 came the second wave of tampering, beginning at J & J and quickly involving several other corporations. The crisis team again, with statesmanship, faced the issue, putting public safety ahead of all other considerations. Capsules, susceptible to tampering, were removed and replaced with caplets; and Tylenol continues to meet the customers' needs.

Moralizing decisions pays off for both a Herb Taylor with a small vital company or a Jim Burke with a large international corporation. Montesquieu, the French philosopher and historian, wrote: "In the infancy of society, the chiefs of state shape institutions, and later the institutions shape the chiefs of state."

Jim Burke told us at FMI Mid-Year 1986 that he long harbored the belief that the most successful corporations with outstanding long-term results are driven by simple moral imperatives: "Serving the public in the broadest possible sense better than their competition."

In the light of the Tylenol tragedies, Jim attempted to uncover convincing evidence to support the contention of moral imperatives in corporate decisions. He looked at corporations that had been in existence for at least thirty years and had credos spelling out their central dedication of serving the public. Also, he wanted assurance from the CEOs that the corporations had lived by their credos for at least a generation.

His staff, working with the Business Round Table and the Ethics Research Center, found twenty-six companies that met the criteria. The compound growth of these firms was 10.7 percent over the thirty years, which was 1.34 times the growth of our GNP, and GNP is ten times greater than it was thirty years ago. The net income of these companies was 21.2 percent greater than average. If thirty years ago you had invested $30,000 in the composite of the Dow Jones, your return would be $134,000 today. For those companies that Jim Burke studied, your $30,000 would have earned a return of $1,310,714.

Moralizing decisions is a leader's hedge for long-term corporate health.

V. COMPROMISE

If there is any part of decision making we have trouble handling, it is compromise. On the frontier we had a habit of admiring people like Bill Travis who drew an uncrossable line at the Alamo. We equate compromise with weakness and certainly a lack of morality.

My own Phoenician bartering background assures me that compromise is a sign of the holistic leader. It indicates that the leader is neither defensive nor compelled to flex his muscles at every challenge.

If there is the need for a decision and conflicting opinions emerge, compromise can work. Compromise isn't reaching the least common denominator thereby making your company impotent. Compromise means strengthening the decision by refining each colleague's area of expertise. Many times compromise is knocking off the rough edges and smoothing the action.

At IGA, I enjoy sifting my ideas through the fertile minds of our teams. I bring in the germ of an idea, knowing each officer is far more knowledgeable in his area of responsibility than I am. What I am after is not pride of authorship but course correction and corporate effectiveness. Such dialogue allows each to carry his weight, and my role is to homogenize our thinking. It has been well said that there is no measuring how much can be accomplished if we are not concerned about who gets the credit.

Warren McCain of Albertson's gained the attention of his key associates when, with tongue in cheek, he sent a memo to them suggesting it would be appropriate if he reduced their salaries by a modest 50 percent! He reminded them they were brought on board to solve problems, but all they were doing was identifying problems.

To be sure, knowing the problem is the first step in correcting a difficult situation, but the knowledge is dangerous if it is left lying on the desk because we lack the courage to decide. Seeing the needs, Warren McCain wrote, earned his associates 50 percent of their pay. Contributing their best thinking to forming the decisions to be made earned them the other half of their salary.

Warren's memo reminded me of a speech by Fred W. Friendly, formerly president of CBS News. Fred described his wife as the finest fifth-grade teacher that God ever created. Her advice to her students is a classic, "The agony of decision-making is so intense that you can only escape it by thinking and acting."

J. Walter Thompson became the world's biggest advertising agency under the leadership of Stanley Resor. He is identified by David Ogilvy as the Brahmin of the advertising business. "Stanley Resor," Mr. Ogilvy wrote, "managed by consensus or compromise. He distrusted individual opinion and he thought brilliance was dangerous."

Blended thinking, of course, isn't insurance against failure, but if the decision proves ineffective, the blame at least can be shared. Leaders abide by the principles of sharing the glory and personally accepting the failures. However, the proper use of compromise is an important step in sound decisions.

VI. ENERGIZE

"Unless a capacity for thinking be accompanied by the capacity for action, a superior mind exists in torture," wrote Benedetto Croce. Will Rogers said, "Even if you're on the right track, you'll get run over if you just sit there." Lee Iacocca would add, "Even a right decision is wrong if made too late."

In High Point, North Carolina, Sid Gayle presides over the largest commercial photography studio under one roof. When I asked him the biggest challenge in managing the creative force, he replied, "They can quickly reach a decision, Tom, but they tend to beat it to death with second-guessing before they act."

Henri-Frederic Amiel would respond, "The man who insists upon seeing with perfect clearness before he decides never decides."

It has been called the paralysis of analysis.

Nothing can energize a company more quickly than a leader's making a courageous decision.

When you feel compatible with the quality of the decision and you match it with effective execution, you then have the alpha and omega of efficiency. You can act with finality, forging ahead with enthusiasm because you have accepted that the buck stops at your desk. The action will depend on how much you value the decision you have made.

Have the Guts to Follow a Hunch

To recap, there is no formula for decision making. Leaders don't count steps before they decide. All I have reported are the signposts I observed most leaders using one way or another. The glue is always intuition linked with courage. John Mikalasky said to a group of students at the New Jersey Institute of Technology: "If something goes beyond the logic that we understand, we say, 'Forget it.' The biggest roadblock to intuitive decision making is not having the guts to follow a good hunch."

We cannot finish our thinking about decision making without commenting about handling the decisions that go sour. "Zeus does not bring all men's plans to fulfillment," said Homer. Sophocles wrote centuries ago in *Antigone*, "All men make mistakes, but a good man yields when he knows his course is wrong, and repairs the evil. The only sin is pride."

We can't always make good decisions but even those that don't give us the desired results are often beneficial. "Experience is the name everyone gives to his mistakes," observed Oscar Wilde. No leader is pleased to make wrong decisions, but he cuts the losses and goes on.

Addressing a convocation at upbeat Pepperdine University, I told the students I got through college on a baseball scholarship, failing two out of three times. Still, batting .333 was more than adequate. Fortunately I was talking about my batting average and not academic results. Then I added that I didn't feel my percentage in business decisions was much better. President Emeritus Howard White, whom I greatly admire, asked me if I didn't misspeak. No, when I consider even little elements like letters I rewrite or calls made again because of a change in thinking, I doubt that my decision-making average is any higher than my hitting average was.

That's why I chuckle when people ask me if I'm a "positive thinker." If you are never negative, how do you know whether you are positive? Don Marquis said it: "An optimist is a guy who has never had much experience." Oh, yes, I can accept positive thinking as Dr. Peale wrote of it in his classic, decades ago, but if you mean "Be giddy," then leave me out.

The late distinguished Congressman Mendel Rivers gave me marvelous advice when he proclaimed, "You don't learn much from the second kick of a mule." The first kick can serve as a Phi Beta Kappa education, but if we require a second kick, we are stupid!

No, I don't know leaders who are proud of bad decisions. They attempt to make each decision good, but the fear of mistakes doesn't inhibit their action. During a summer at college, I picked peaches for Mr. Clements of Holly Springs, South Carolina. One night a storm blew through the orchard, bending the trees to the ground. The next morning Mr. Clements surveyed the damage and said, "Boys, all we can do is cut down the trees, pull up the stumps, burn them, and replant the orchard; but before we do, let's be sure we've plucked off every good peach."

The leader has his storms, his private hells. In fact, it is his scars that make us identify with him.

The wagon master found tough decisions had to be made before leaving St. Louis, and even making the hard decisions didn't guarantee safe, successful passage. Leaders, too, do the best their experience and intuition have taught them.

6

It's in the Stars

Did you ever peer over Ward Bond's shoulder and see his wagon master's map? Maps usually are the result of survey-ing, measuring, and mathematical reckoning. But the wagon master's was as much a report as it was a map. It was a dog-eared collection of notes, charts, and scribbling about the last trip; a combination of log, diary, and map held together with much pride of authorship, it proved to the "pilgrims" that the wagon master had made it West—and back—before.

All maps were suspect, for much could happen to the terrain between journeys. A rainfall could redirect a river wiping out a ford marked on the map. A rock slide could seal a strategic canyon pass; the movement of an Indian tribe could detour the wagons around a favored sweet grass prairie. So in joining any wagon train, the pilgrims showed great confi-dence in the wagon master's ability to negotiate with nature and innovate with available resources. They trusted the man, not the map.

For his part, the wagon master knew that although the route could change, the hardships encountered would be consis-tent. He could remember the last group of pilgrims when they ascended the Rockies. The precious heirlooms they had hoarded and hid from him in St. Louis were unceremoniously dumped overboard. All tangible mementos from back East, or the world before, rolled heartbreakingly down the hillside. But weight had to be reduced and time was of the essence.

On the other side of South Pass, the wagon master had to

make a strategic decision: either continue on to Fort Bridger for rest and resupply, or dash north eighty-five miles through the alkali barrenness of Sublette's Cutoff and gain a week of time. The wagons were traveling a maximum of ten miles a day now and it was September.

Amidst the autumn blaze at Fort Hall, the wagon master had to make the last irrevocable choice. Time was precious; he had to be right! He would have liked easier options than going south 525 miles through the Great Salt Basin and over the Sierras, or striking out north through Snake River country, across the Blue Mountains and down the wild Columbia River, another 230 miles. Either way, there was that deadline— make it before November or not make it at all.

The call always was his. Sure, he listened to his scouts and heard the rumors circulating at the way stations; but he had to exercise the option. No wonder far more time was spent gazing, meditating, thinking under the stars than in rereading the map. While the pilgrims escaped into sleep, he pondered the heavens. In his gut he felt the answer; his starting out again meant he knew he was right.

Developing the Brilliance of Intuitive Leadership

The wagon master was not unlike the leader of today's frontier. He makes quantum leaps which later will be reduced to logical steps. Recognized for his stability, the leader is hard-pressed to explain the apparent rashness of his action. The leap is fraught with risk, but a greater danger would be doing nothing. Nature has a cruel law: "Stop and I'll kill you." Keep a bush from spreading and it withers. Keep a bud from bursting and it dies. There is no "Fort Status Quo."

That is why it is so difficult to define leadership. How do you make sense of flashes of insight, bold strokes of action, slashing cuts through red tape? Managers can direct the procedures once agreed upon, holding in check their own intuitive impulses. But the leader is 180 degrees opposite. While computers spit out statistics, while research teams ferret out the facts, while consultants introduce their "What if's?" the leader must initiate innovation. The more complex the challenge, the greater the risk-reward ratio, the more true it seems that only the leader's raw intuition can trigger the solution.

Now, my intention is not to downplay managers. They manage the day-by-day as well as perfect intuitive action. Also, in many instances, they are held in check by a too closely defined job description.

Ashley Montague, I believe, called it corporate "psycho-sclerosis" which he defined as "a rigidity of mind that defies intuition." Here is one of the breakdowns of the average MBA program that relies solely on the "case method" of teaching. The case method is simply an illustration of the past, not a pattern for the future. The MBA must not cite cases as a lawyer would for legal precedence. Precedence must not automatically become procedure.

Dr. Henry Mintzbert of McGill University sees the leader as a "holistic, intuitive thinker who constantly relies on hunches to cope with problems far too complex for rational analysis." Dr. Abraham Marlow sees leaders as eagles on flights of imagination, making resolutions that disregard the anticipated.

Philosopher Karl Popper would even go a step farther in his belief: "There is no such thing as a logical method of having new ideas, or a logical reconstruction of this process. Every discovery contains an 'irrational element.' Maybe that's what we meant when as kids we said we'd 'feel it in our funny bone.'"

I am not suggesting that innovation is a gift for a privileged few. It isn't. But like all gifts, it must be accepted and appropriated to our use. The late Walt Disney said the gift was made operative when accompanied by the four C's: curiosity, confidence, courage, and constancy. Prioritizing, he placed confidence as the most important.

Intuitive leadership is not being mystic as much as being a hard worker with an open mind. The problems of American industry do not result from our dollar being strong or not, but from our lack of basic competitiveness in world markets. Our productivity suffers not from improper tools but from an evasion of reality so complete that one wonders if sizable chunks of America's basic industries are salvageable, regardless of our currency problems.

Intuitive thinking begins with a knowledgeable search through all that is known about a problem. Right here some CEOs never rise to leadership. For in their "hotdogging" it, they are unwilling to invest the time, capital, and work to review the existing prices, demographically comprehend the market, or recognize who the competition is and what they are doing. A thorough systematic search establishes present status. Like all of God's gifts, intuitive insights only come in pushing on to the frontier.

Intuition by its very definition doesn't always accommodate our time scheme. We can't push a button. The more we force intuition, the further it flies from us. Try to forcefully grab intuition, and all you will get is a fistful of feathers. Pretenders try to glue feathers on themselves to fly; the results are an embarrassing corporate crash landing.

The intuition that we applaud at the point of crisis is actually developed in solitude: mulling, considering, toying. (It is my conviction that God never makes a soul stand tall publicly which hasn't for a time, been tutored privately.) St. Paul was in the desert of Arabia before he was recognized as the leader of the early church. One of the reasons I have never chafed under my flying schedule of one thousand air miles daily over the last two decades is the protected time it provides for my mind to freewheel. Cultivating our intuition is unchaining ourselves from the obvious: "How would I act if I rejected what has been suggested as the obvious solution? . . . If I could remove the fences my accountant or lawyer has built around me, what would be my answer? . . . Is it possible I'm letting the rules dictate to me instead of their being the parameters of my freedom?"

In 1953 J. D. Watson and F. H. C. Crick were facing a thorny problem. They wanted to know the organic chemical make-up of the molecular structure encoding all our genetic traits. They had to consider the rules of genetics, the body of chemistry, molecular laws, and biological science. Though they were well aware of all these disciplines and their interaction, they asked of themselves, "If we weren't burdened by all these rules, what would our answer look like—ideally?" Well, ideally, they reasoned, if they didn't have to consider all the current rules, it would be a double helix consisting of a pair of polynucleotides coiled together. This is what they searched for. They found DNA. Little wonder they were honored with the Nobel Prize.

So when I see the leader as having intestinal fortitude, I am not writing of brute strength or a bully pulpit but "gut feelings," the courage to act on hunches, unwillingness to rest on laurels or play it safe. The leader is aware that what you don't use, you lose. I remember well when I broke my right wrist as a lad and had to learn to write all over again when the cast was removed. My hand had lost the power to write and had to be retaught.

A leader knows better than to blunt his intuitive feelings. It takes confidence to activate a nonintellectual answer that feels eminently correct. Always, there rings in the back of my mind a word of advice given to me September of 1956. I was moving from Rock Hill, South Carolina, to a new parish in High Point, North Carolina. Like any new opportunity, it gave me a chance to begin anew. My youthful zeal had often outrun my knowledge and experience in Rock Hill, but still God had miraculously blessed our congregation. Dr. Henry Pope Mobley, the respected senior minister of Oakland Avenue Presbyterian Church, had been my "father confessor" when I realized some of my outrageous blunders.

He put his hand on my shoulder in a farewell comment: "Tom, you'll grow and mature, but as you do, there comes a tendency to become too cautious. Whatever you do, don't lose your audacity. Don't reject your basic instincts. Don't play it safe, or you'll just succumb to a sameness, tameness, and lameness."

The open leader has the additional problem of trying to explain the workability of his actions. Although I say that intuition doesn't make you a mystic, at times you will be labeled mystical because you can't at the moment explain or justify your burst of insight. It's just another aspect of the loneliness of leadership, and you hope you have earned the followers' trust.

I recognize the computer's help in quickly gathering facts, enabling better allocation of resources, quickly identifying demographic changes, reducing the time needed for routine matters, and monitoring corporate performance. But the computer, totally logical and absolutely rational, can't address the problems awaiting creativity, intuition, and hunches. The computer arrives at its answer with blinding speed but also with metaphysical predictability. It has never heard of imagination and can't conceive nonlogical relationships. The computer doesn't possess spirituality, emotions, enthusiasm, or humor.

Milliken and Company: "Our Greatest Asset . . . Our People . . . Our Goal . . . An Unquenchable Thirst to Be the Best

Because of my fascination with intuitive leadership, I have shadowed Roger Milliken almost from the day he assumed the helm of his family-owned textile company in 1947.

Of all people, I was the least surprised when *Business Week* identified Roger Milliken as "one of the nation's most powerful but unpublicized industrialists." He is "decidedly unflamboyant" but gives a shining face to textiles which is, as a basic industry, woefully understated and too often unappreciated. No U.S. industry can equal the productivity record of textiles.

Despite his modesty, Roger has become a headliner in business periodicals and books, but I feel his intuitive leadership is still not fully comprehended, which limits just how helpful he can be as a role model.

For a point of reference, let me first give you a statistical overview: Milliken & Company (the name since 1976, previously Deering Milliken) is over one hundred years old, pegging its beginning in 1865 as a dry goods jobber in Portland, Maine. Seth Milliken, Roger's grandfather, was the founder. When Roger was born in 1915, the company had moved to New York City and become involved in financing manufacturing suppliers which later led to the acquisition of their mills.

Roger had a typical and proper Park Avenue raising, culminating in graduation from Yale in 1937. His classmates included Downing Jenks, John Murchison, Perry Bass, Rogers Morton, Potter Stewart, Henry Becton, and John Field. This was the infamous class that Yale's dean predicted would fail but which probably holds the record for recognized leaders.

During the fifties and sixties, the textile headlines were held by J.P. Stevens' acquisition binge and Spenser Love's explosive growth which resulted in the sprawling and somewhat unmanageable Burlington Industries.

Milliken was quietly enlarging its base to 40 plants. Today, while the other national textile firms retrench and merge, Milliken continues its steady growth. For instance, in the first half of 1985, Milliken used 349 different fibers to produce 1,065 fabric styles featuring 10,552 custom colors in their product line including clothing, uniforms, carpet, automobile interiors, drapery, wallcovering, and chemicals.

The company does have the advantage and flexibility of being family owned. Years ago, one of Franklin Roosevelt's trusted business advisors, Adolf Berle, Jr., joined Gardiner C. Means in writing *The Modern Corporation and Private Property*. The book's thesis: the management of American business had undergone a significant change. No longer were our large corporations run by founders, by owners, or by entrepreneurs but by professional managers who had minimum stakes in the equity. On the other side, I have also seen the demise of family companies as they have become spoiled, tentative, and reticent as they devolved from one generation to another.

Either way, the scarce resources today are leadership, knowledge, vision, acceptance of change, recognizing people's needs, and the ability to work together—all the strength that is not found on the balance sheet.

Roger Milliken is a 10 as a progressive, intuitive leader. If you read the current verbiage about him, you would get the impression that in 1978 when he took one of his infrequent vacations, he just tossed into his briefcase Philip B. Cosby's book, *Quality Is Free*, read it, and stormed down the mountains with new tablets of command for Milliken & Company. Wrong! In fairness, if you took the theoretical premises of *Quality Is Free* without the pragmatic realism of Milliken & Company's years of experience, your starting dream could move rapidly to a nightmare.

Like all leaders, Roger believes the leader must be the eternal student. Phil Cosby's book gave orderliness and curriculum to what Roger believed but hadn't reduced to an agenda.

Milliken & Company didn't change direction in 1978; they uncovered a better trail to reach their frontier. The decision "to move out and go West" Roger made in 1939, and he may not even know its drama.

Recruiting two textile engineers from Philadelphia, he established modest living quarters in his Excelsor Mill in Union, South Carolina, a long way from home for a Park Avenue "Yalee." He lived right in the factory that fried in the summer heat and froze in the winter! While others bragged of the value of their employees from the safe distance of their executive suites, Roger came to know his people personally—their needs and desires and their dedication to their labor.

Yes, Roger wanted to know *them*, not just *about* them! He wanted to see the interplay; he wanted to hear the thumping of their hearts. He became a part of their lives. Not to be cute, but in Union, South Carolina, Roger Milliken learned to walk in union with the employees, to feel their hurts, to understand their ambitions for their children. He felt the burdens that led them to their local churches in the mill village and the burdens that drove them to escape for a "lost weekend." He viewed the weddings, celebrated the births, and wept at the funerals. He saw the first Gold Stars in their living room windows and felt with his people the sad loss of a son at Pearl Harbor. Most importantly, the shuttlecock of the looms beat a theme that captured Roger's total commitment: if he could lead, he had inherited an employee family capable of being the best.

He reduced his commitment to a simple math: create an atmosphere where people feel good about themselves; show how good you feel about them by the equipment you provide for production; and they will reward you with high productivity.

The intuitive leader understands you can't expect people to perform any better than your willingness to invest in their skills.

As soon as World War II was over and Roger was at the helm, he made his eloquent statement of how much he valued the employees. At Clemson, South Carolina, a town better known for producing football players than bolts of cloth, he built a state-of-the-art, totally air-conditioned mill. A new day for textiles!

Now let's leap forward to today and visit Roger Milliken, flanked by his young president, Tom Malone. Tom is typical of a leader's associate choices. He is anything but a clone. Graduated with honors (Ph.D. in chemistry) from Georgia Tech and the product of Milliken & Company's policy of recruiting the best from the campus, Tom understands the Milliken culture. Milliken employees are rewarded highly and are only too happy to work twenty-hour days when necessary. They're enthusiastic about seven-day weeks when there is a job to be finished. They know you're guilty of stealing from the company if you're reticent to think creatively.

Every time I see Roger and Tom, I am reminded of the elder Caleb and the younger Joshua in the Old Testament. Moses sent twelve men to check out the land of Canaan to see whether the people of Israel could survive in the land and whether the present inhabitants of the land were good or bad. Ten of the spies came back and said that the land was prosperous, that there was great potential but Israel was too weak to compete. It wouldn't be an "even playing field!" (That's a phrase you have read in many a business magazine.) The people looked like giants in their eyes. Caleb, with the strength that comes with age, and Joshua, with the vigor of youth, agreed that obstacles would confront them, but they saw the land as potential "milk and honey" that the people of Israel could obtain if they had a single purpose.

Now you can understand why I honor Roger and Tom. While other manufacturers wilt before the potential offshore giants, Milliken & Company believes that there is still "milk and honey" in textiles.

This isn't blind optimism. No company has studied the giants such as Japan more than Milliken. They sent twenty of their key executives to observe the plants there and get to know their counterparts. At least every six months Tom Malone or one of his senior officers visits Japan for an update. They have reached a simple conclusion: they can't do it exactly like the Japanese but they can be just as effective.

In fact, Honda in Marysville, Kentucky, and Nissan in Smyrna, Tennessee, have proven to be the most profitable plants of these particular Japanese corporations. In a visit in early 1986, fourteen key Japanese CEOs said they were coming to the United States without any prioritized patents, no inside secrets, yet they knew they could increase profits if they could place a plant here in the States. This indicated to Roger and Tom that there is nothing wrong with America's people, only with the way that our companies are run.

A curiosity. If you ask Roger Milliken the secret of his company's strength today, you would think that you were hearing an echo from his 1947 answer: "Our greatest asset . . . our people. Our goal . . . an unquenchable thirst to be the best."

Haven't you heard almost every executive up or down, such as Alfred Sloan of GM, say something like: "Take my plants, rob my assets, but leave me my people, and we'll rise again"? It's everybody's preaching: it's a practice of a select few.

So how does giant Milliken do it today? It is, of course, no longer possible for Roger Milliken to walk out on the plant floors as he did at the Excelsor plant in Union, but he still knows his people face to face. In the "Care Room," he has the 4,000 managers of the 16,000 employees of Milliken pictured. Then with typical stamina, Roger and Tom for six consecutive weeks annually—and at least six days a week for a minimum of 10 hours daily—study each face, asking Bruce Corbett, vice president of personnel, and the other officers to fill them in on the individual's career path. What is he doing now; what should he be doing tomorrow? This is not managing by wandering around, but it is living with the people.

In the monthly presidents' meeting, twelve key executives spend the first 40 percent of the two-day meeting discussing personnel, sometimes spending all the time on personnel until they are satisfied they have the right executive in the right slot. Contrast this with most such meetings that would spend 90 percent on financials and 10 percent on personnel. Their meetings are just the reverse, for after they deal with personnel, they talk about their quality standards, with the last moments reserved for financials.

With every confidence, Milliken & Company believes that if a company creates an atmosphere where the employee gets a sense of achievement from quality work, then the financials take care of themselves.

Quality of Service and Work are Their Own Reward

We do believe this, don't we? The second job I had was delivering newspapers for *The Brockton Enterprise*. Living in Holbrook, Massachusetts, I had a choice of delivering one of the half-dozen Boston papers of that day or the *Enterprise*. I chose the *Enterprise* for one simple reason: they paid a half cent more per paper than did the Boston papers.

The Brockton paper paid half a cent more, not because they cared more about their newspaper carriers, but because we could not throw the paper up into the yard. We had to secure it behind a screen or storm door or under a mat.

Today, if my newspaper boy didn't throw my paper in the yard, I'd miss half my exercise! Each day when I turn in the drive, I try to determine what new and creative spot the carrier is using this time. I always start in the wettest part of the yard and move from there. *The Brockton Enterprise* took pride in saying, "You always receive your paper in readable condition." And I learned the important principle: *Quality of Service and Work Has Its Own Reward.*

Oh, I should finish the story, for if I don't put in the next part, you would miss the whole point. The Brockton paper also had scrambled routes rather than protected routes, meaning that in this little community of 1,000 people and at most 250 homes, we had five paper routes. It meant that on any given street, three different newspaper people might be serving three consecutive houses. Customers were kept by quality service.

The test of quality is what you do right under the pressure of competition.

Translated to Milliken decision makers, the story would be something like this. They recruit the best people possible. They try to promote from within; and at the same time they use an elaborate array of consultants —not the headliners but the most astute in their fields because Milliken leaders don't

98

want the destructiveness of inbreeding and do want constant updating. It also means that they don't hoard profits but commission twelve key officers to scour the world for the latest equipment. If equipment is needed but cannot be located, Milliken leaders turn them loose to use their R&D department to manufacture it. See what I am writing—they turn loose their key executives.

Intuitive leadership gives birth to more intuitive leadership, allowing executives to handle a project from beginning to end, giving them responsibility for the bottom line. Thus within the company freestanding businesses exist under the umbrella, with the president of each division feeling that he has his own company but reporting to the corporation president, Malone, and chairman, Milliken.

Bruce Atwater, Jr., of General Mills has spelled it out by saying, "Our goal is to make each Profit Center Manager feel like a CEO of his particular business activity." When given this responsibility, the divisional presidents with their teams will then turn loose their creative juices, which usually means more frugal spending.

Quality just doesn't happen, nor can it be left unmonitored. With Phil Cosby's advice, Milliken attacked vehemently the age-old problem of "seconds," that is cloth with just a minor imperfection, using their Error Cause Removal Step. According to Malone, "ECR is the key to allowing every single person in the organization to participate in the quality improvement process, whether they are manufacturing, marketing, styling, development, engineering or support staff." It took four years to get this process under way, but in 1984 they had 8,528 ECRs submitted and 6,891 completed, thereby saving the company over $6 million or about $1 thousand per ECR submitted. The last time I visited with them, they were at a rate of 6,000 ECRs per year.

They coupled the ECRs with their Correction Action Teams, many of which were formed as the result of specific ECRs submitted by their people. In 1984, they completed 1,110 Corrective Action Team projects and saved the company over $20 million.

Tom Malone continues to say, "There is no question that the ECR program is the key ingredient to continual involvement of all associates in our company. It is also clear that 'teams' solve problems much more effectively than individuals! Especially when the teams include those individuals who are directly involved in the process being studied."

Let me add that these improvements are not only inside the plants, but the same approach is also taken to marketing and the sales force. Out of that approach has come computerized shipping so that Milliken can actually stop and divert trucks en route.

This type of thinking brought about the Millitron-design computer which helps interior design firms create in-house carpet and furniture designs. The Millitron uses eight color setups. The computer operating this equipment can make 50 million decisions a minute, and a 9' x 12' area rug in 29 seconds. More speckled than the rainbow in the land of Oz, this technology can literally invent a color, superimpose it on a preexisting photograph or drawing, thus providing virtually instant R&D. Little wonder that twenty thousand corporate visitors toured Milliken to get ideas for their companies, many of which were totally unrelated to textiles.

Let me hasten, though, to clear up some misunderstandings. Milliken does not offer life-long or guaranteed employment—and neither does Japan. However, as Bruce Corbett told me, if a manager has been with the company for twenty-five productive years, they consider he is too valuable as well as too fine an investment for them to lose. In 1982 when they closed some of their aging plants, they placed a group of three hundred surplus managers on special assignments in the remaining fifty plants. Not only did they earn their own salaries, but they saved the company millions of dollars by working on special problems, solving some which have been inherent in the textile industry for years.

Another statement we hear is that in 1978 Roger Milliken finally overcame paternalism. Absolutely wrong again! He is paternal. Absolutely! What's wrong with enlightened paternalism that allows individual expression? In his biography, *Albert Schweitzer's Mission: Healing and Peace* (New York: Norton, 1985), Norman Cousins said, "For better or for worse, [Albert] Schweitzer was a patriarch. I remember saying to him that he was an enlightened despot —to which he replied, 'An enlightened despot is able to give the greatest amount of freedom.'"

Enlightened paternalism actually means that the leader serves the followers. Roger Milliken willingly takes on the role of a servant. He lives modestly. The last time we were together I was amused by the torn pocket on his suit. He resists interviews, and he always takes the greatest corporate risk to himself in the shepherd's role we identified earlier. Whether called a "shepherd" or "paternal" or just "leader," he has accepted the responsibility of the followers. Milliken & Company did not go through a revolution in 1978, but an evolution which is normal to intuitive leaders.

Another myth would be that quality is a philosophy. I beg to differ. Quality is more than that. It is a religion. This is what I tried to explain to my son after he viewed a CBS television show on the Japanese automobile industry on January 29, 1981. It is amazing to me, not that foreign automobiles are successful but that they can get so much free publicity through programs built on one theme: "If you want a good car, go foreign. If you want problems, buy domestic." I wasn't home to watch the program and only saw the closing fifteen or twenty minutes on a television in a hotel room.

When I arrived home the next day, our son, who is an automobile "nut," asked if I saw the program. I told him that I had not. He said, "Well, Dad, may we discuss it?" Anytime our son Allan wants to discuss anything that is even remotely academic, he has Dad's undivided attention.

"Allan, I'm listening," I said.

"Dad," he said, "do you know that in Japan they have homes for the employees to live in? They have recreational fields for the people to play on and a store owned by the corporation from which the employees can make purchases. No wonder they're so successful."

My reply: "Allan, there is no question that the Japanese have their manufacturing at an effective level; but I don't think what you mentioned is the reason for their success. Oh, they do have outstanding plants. When I first started lecturing there in 1964, I was impressed that they could manufacture motorcycles in factories as clean as many of the hospitals of our land. It's true that they have recreation for the employees, homes, and so on.

"Allan, everything you have mentioned, the textile community had half a century ago here in the Southeast; and it was maintained until about twelve years ago when, in the name of social progress, it was eliminated. The reputation of Charles Cannon was raped by those who said he wanted to control the people who worked for him. In fact, my prediction is that the same social planners will someday get to the Japanese, and they too will complain.

"When I came south to go to school, employees had company songs; they lived in company homes. You found some of the finest community fervor anywhere, so I don't think that's the reason for Japan's success.

"Son, to understand any people, you have to understand their religion. That's especially true outside the United States and England. In Japan they basically worship by Shinto discipline. Incorporated in that faith is a wholesome respect for the victor, the strong, the conqueror. Back before World War II, every Cracker Jacks box had a little Japanese toy in the bottom of it. Your grandmother wouldn't allow me to touch it. She knew that if it was from Japan, it was junk. If I played with it, I might even get diseased! Or my eyes might slant; and that certainly wouldn't be a good combination with this large Syrian-Lebanese nose!

"The Japanese went to war and had the Pacific won, but they miscalculated in their strategy. More than that, they underestimated the spirit of our people. They torpedoed our carrier—*Yorktown*; we limped away and then came back to fight another day. We would shoot their zeroes out of the sky, and they wouldn't come back. They would shoot our P-40s down; we'd rebuild and have them flying again. They found that no people fight as courageously as the people who hate war. We combined the strength of our industry with the keenness of our military mind, and we won the war. They respected us.

"Oh, a lot of the people in the clergy thought the Japanese were becoming Christians. No, they weren't giving up the Shinto faith; they just added a Christian hat on top out of respect for us. They began to study us. In general, they are not particularly creative people; but they are the finest of copiers.

"They wanted to find out why we succeeded and why they failed. They saw our quality, and they began to apply it and make it their standard. What did we do? We went to the highest mountains; we smote ourselves on the breasts; we cocked our chins up; we threw our shoulders back and we said, 'We are the best, the finest, the greatest.' We thought we were hearing applause when, actually, it was the echo of our own voices. We became so drunk with our success that it became excess. However, the Japanese had learned the lesson of quality; and it stayed long after our occupation ended.

"Allan, my son, remember this. We never stumble on our weak points; we stumble on our strong points. We carefully guard our flanks of weakness, and we carelessly take for granted our reputation of strength. Look at the Bible to prove this. Moses' strength was his meekness. Where did he fail so that Joshua had to lead the people of Israel into the Promised Land? Moses stumbled over his meekness.

"Elijah the prophet was known for his boldness. Why did Elisha have to take over? Because Elijah became faint-hearted. He stumbled over his boldness. Look at St. Peter. His strong point was his courage. He dared to walk on the water. In a moment of anguish, he took a borrowed sword and cut off the ear of the high priest. He said that though every disciple would leave Jesus, he would never leave. Yet who was it that cursed on three occasions and said he never even knew who Jesus was? It was the same Simon Peter.

"Son, you could beat your dad very simply in tennis; but I continue to win because I guard my weak points. If I do fail, it's usually because I get careless with what I know how to do best.

"Allan, quality just doesn't drop down from the ceiling at a certain time in your life. Quality in later life begins now, with the way you go back to your room and study your algebra."

He went back to his room; I doubt it was to study algebra but probably to watch another rerun of *Wonder Woman*, which you'll have to admit was the best Linda Carter ever looked.

That's what it's all about. You see, quality is the test of your integrity. Quality is how faithful you are to the talents God has given you. Even work, in essence, is holy. Work is nothing more than the stage upon which you display your talents.

▮▮▮

Hopefully, I have made clear why I have selected the title "It's in the Stars." Intuitive leaders historically outperform those who wait upon factual confirmation or conventional wisdom. There are no textbooks for the intuitive leader. We need willed and diligent commitment. We need to use our free will to make courageous decisions. We must be so committed to employee and customer that the necessity of helping them does become the "Mother of Invention."

Let me rest my case on this statement by our highest-ranked Vietnam POW, Admiral James B. Stockdale:

> A leader must aspire to a strength, a compassion and a conviction several octaves above that required by society in general. Glib and detached people can get by in positions of authority until the pressure is on. When the crunch develops, people cling to those whom they can trust.

7

Wagon Master—First Among Equals

No matter what part of the country the pioneers came from, until they got to one of the western "jumping-off" points, they traveled pretty much on their own. Down the Ohio by boat, across Illinois and Indiana via turnpike, up the Missouri River or overland from Council Bluffs, Iowa, the company of western travelers was never really formed until they hit Independence, Westport, St. Joe, or later, Ft. Leavenworth in Kansas.

All of the pioneers shared the same goal of going to Oregon, and their company would need a set of rules on the trail set by a leader who functioned much like a captain on a ship.

So at a general meeting of all the company, nominations for captain or wagon master would spring forth from the group and an election would be held. One man would be called forth to lead even as he would remain an associate and fellow pioneer.

Committees could be established to advise and counsel the wagon master but final decisions henceforth would remain in his hands.

The wagon master set the hours for leaving each morning (usually 7:00 A.M.); when and where they would stop for noon meal and the same for evening camp. Each man was required to do watch duty, which began at 8:00 P.M. and ended at 5:00 the next morning. One day in seven was a day of rest.

Each person's place in the wagon train was decided by the wagon master, and any other rules that he and his committee decided were necessary became law; violations incurred punishment which could range from reprimand to hanging, though being expelled from the wagon train was normally the most severe. Only forgiveness by the entire company could allow a violator to reenter the train.

The wagon master's day began at 5:00 A.M. in the morning and ended at 8:00 P.M. He was allowed no special privileges, was not paid, and served at the pleasure of the company. For this exalted position, he took all the abuse and complaints the pioneers could give, over everything from broken wheel spokes to unpredictable weather.

He made the whole thing work by enthusiasm and enterprise that never failed when the going got tough.

Spirit is hard to define and even more difficult to design. Corporations, much like wagon trains, roll on by the direction of a wagon master; but those directions must match up with the desires of the people. The resulting chemistry we call "spirit."

In the last chapter, we watched Roger Milliken move in with his people so that he might understand who they were and what they were about. He never felt for a moment that the employees should meet him halfway but, rather, that he should go to where they were if he was to lead them where they both wanted to go.

Richard D. Harrison, chairman of the Fleming Companies, has built the largest wholesale distribution corporation whose only product is food. Dick was a pioneer thirty years ago in initiating what is now becoming popular—that is, calling his 18,000 employees "associates." He not only has *called* them associates, but also has *made* them associates. The associates are supported not by shareholders but by stakeholders.

To the Fleming Companies the associates approach is everything but a fad. Companies that are romanced by buzz word terminology make using the word *associates* a fad and not a fact. I know when you visited your local bookstore last, you saw again how Americans are hooked on simplistic self-improvement manuals that run the gamut from undisciplined dieting, to overnight millions in real estate, to management by new labels. Over the last quarter century, managers' hopes have been built and then dashed on an unbelievable number of schemes that assured corporate success without sacrifice.

106

In fact, the more scientific the term used, the more suspect the results. Given the pressures of contemporary business where "nothing is easy anymore," fads become the "executive Valium" of the haggard manager reeling in the face of risky decision making that can make or break a company. In the frustrating search for the safe and secure, a "sedative fad" becomes the next best thing. However, the system quickly builds up an immunity so that the sedative repeatedly must be replaced with stronger potions. In that twilight zone before the next quick fix, it would be well to be sobered by the reality that anything worthwhile takes effort and the drying out process to become "fad-free" is usually gory before glory.

Ned Fleming, the last living architect of the sixty-year-old IGA stores, originated the upside-down management approach; that is, the person you work for is not to be viewed as your "boss" but the person to go to for help. The people have the solution; leadership consists in energizing it.

This solid company with 650 employees and gross annual sales of $62.5 million recruited Dick Harrison in 1953. Encasing a philosophy in a process was to be Dick's destiny, and what a destiny it has become! After a decade as executive vice president, Dick assumed the helm of a company doing $313 million in sales and profits better than $2.5 million. (Keep in mind earning 1 percent on sales is the ultimate for wholesale food distribution companies.) Today, a quarter of a century later and viewing 18,000 employees as "associates," Fleming Companies will exceed $8 billion in sales and realize profits exceeding $60 million.

I discovered Dick's management style while viewing his newly completed automated warehouse in Oklahoma City. Never before had I seen cartons of food flying along the various tracks to be assembled in orderly fashion for loading into one of the many trucks. Dick and I paused and watched the man controlling the movement with his computer panel at the cloverleaf of the various tracks. We arrived just moments before he would rotate off. The intense responsibility made periodic breaks a necessity.

As the operator turned the controls over to a fellow worker, Dick introduced him to me and said, "Tom, I want you to meet one of my associates." You talk about a contrast, there was a contrast! Dick, in his buttoned-down style, always dressed like the finest corporate executive, standing by a man in a personalized T-shirt and scrubbed safety shoes who had bulging muscles developed before automation and long, tousled hair. I thought it was gracious for Dick to call him an "associate," but mentally I questioned the exaggeration.

As we continued through the Oklahoma City Distribution Center, it finally hit me that his was not a placating word nor the reflection of a written philosophy, but it was indeed a practice resulting from the attitude of Dick Harrison and his corporate team.

In the Fleming vocabulary, associate means teamwork and cooperation, a spirit of mutual trust and respect, a shared commitment to strategy and mission, a coordination of common goals, and an individual's acceptance of responsibility. To Dick and his colleagues in the executive offices, leadership for Fleming did not result because they are #1 in size; but because of the commitment of their associates whose human needs are met and whose expectations are fulfilled through their work experience.

Fleming invests in automation not to reduce the labor count but rather to increase sales so that more people have an opportunity to be associated with the company. What I thought was a hopelessly optimistic gesture and a vain attempt to be democratic, was really working.

As I write these pages, the food industry faces a serious test. It is in a period of food deflation. Fleming not only faces this, but its basic area of service includes the devastated farm belt. During the inflationary Carter era, food companies enjoyed the advantage of safe forward buying. With a healthy cash flow, they could stuff their warehouses, knowing whatever entered would exit at an increased price or bargain. The economic terms, LIFO and FIFO, became understandable even to the layman. Deflation challenges any boast about productivity, efficiency, and competitiveness. It strips away facade and exaggeration leaving us naked and exposed. Much like the wagon train, we have left the comfortable plains to challenge the rugged mountains.

The Fleming earnings record is impacted by today's onslaught. In the long term, however, Fleming will continue to achieve productivity and effectiveness. Its employees, you see, are not performing jobs but are associates sharing responsibilities.

What in Dick Harrison's background would have led him to institute the associates approach? Meet him: Salt-Lake-City-born, an honor graduate from Stanford University with a law degree from the University of Michigan, sedate and debonair.

Even if I were a child psychologist, I would be reluctant to explain why some children question while others seek the anonymity within the herd. Motherless at an early age, Dick was raised by two doting aunts and a caring but severe father whose respect he longed to gain but not at the price of just "going along to get along." As a Cub Scout—that would climax with his Eagle Scout designation years later—Dick once stood with his right hand uplifted to declare the Cub Scout oath, only to be reminded by his agnostic father, "We don't believe in God."

With conviction and love competing for his loyalty, Dick whispered to himself, "Maybe you don't Father, but I do." Early on the pressures of popularity would not deafen his ear to his own drummer.

"Life is what happens to you while you're busy making other plans" is more than a song line. Enthusiastically responding to his country's call during World War II, Dick became a B-29 pilot. Before the responsibility of command, he flew shotgun with an overbearing major who never introduced his crew by name, but with haughtiness, swagger, and braggadocio, snarled about *"my* co-pilot"; *"my* navigator"; *"my* engineer"; *"my* bombardier." Flooding Dick's mind was the resolution, "If and when I'm given a B-29 to command, I'll introduce our crew by name, including the ground crew!" He became one of the, if not *the,* youngest B-29 command pilot flying missions over Japan.

After his B-29 had dumped its payload on Japan and was clear of the antiaircraft zone, Dick Harrison had thinking time during the long ride back. If he was fortunate enough to survive the war, he would fly his B-29 "associates-philosophy" into the private sector. A daring idea. Remember that the accepted executive practice after the war was: "Locate the influential among *my* work force; sell them *my* program; achieve *my* goals."

General F. C. "Red" Gideon was my U.S. Air Force mentor. General Gideon's progressive "wing" view was that crew chiefs and ground personnel should be treated with respect equal to the pilots. He viewed the entire Air Force as airmen, all responsible, with the insignia of rank identifying the level of responsibility.

As Roger Milliken sought to understand his employees, Dick Harrison sought to understand himself and his associates by assuming his associates had similar needs. It was more than walking in another's sandals. It was allowing another the space to walk, even on your path. This philosophy echoes the words of Clarence Francis, the builder of General Foods: "You can buy a man's time; you can buy his physical presence at a given place; you can buy a measured number of his skilled muscular motions per hour. But you cannot buy enthusiasm. You cannot buy loyalty. You cannot buy devotion of hearts, minds or souls. You must earn these."

Frustration? I guarantee it if you try to copy the actions of a Roger Milliken or a Dick Harrison. Fun, I promise, if you get in step with their attitude. Here is where fad books fail. They tend to tell the head what to do instead of convincing the heart what to believe.

The ultimate description of the "associate" approach is in the Bible. The Apostle Paul writes in the second chapter of his letter to the Philippians:

> Fulfill my joy by being like-minded, having the same love, being of one accord, of one mind. Let nothing be done through selfish ambition or conceit, but in lowliness of mind let each esteem others better than himself. Let each of you look out not only for his own interests, but also for the interests of others. Let this mind be in you which was also in Christ Jesus, who, being in the form of God, did not consider it robbery to be equal with God, but made Himself of no reputation, taking the form of a servant, and coming in the likeness of

men. . . . Therefore God also has highly exalted Him. . . .

The "Associates Approach" and Productivity

Assuming we have the "associates" attitude, then, we are ready for our philosophy to be encased in a process; but the process only has validity when the attitude is correct.

Dick Harrison recruited Dick Williams to serve as Executive Vice President, Human Resources. The title sounds good but, more important, Dick Williams doesn't report through a chain of command but flanks Dick Harrison with direct communication.

One of the fiercest debates of my career was in 1975 when I introduced the associates approach to Scouting. One of our board members took me on. He saw personnel as merely a staff function. The rebirth of Scouting was almost stopped at that moment, but wiser heads prevailed.

The associate concept is only disgusting flattery if it is not the greatest asset a company enjoys. Only associates who feel like associates bring about the dramatic productivity gains the Fleming Companies enjoy.

Unless productivity is surrounded by the proper culture, it takes on a crude image. It seems to say that I, as an employer, can use you as an employee, to make me look good. Reread the leading business periodicals of the last half dozen years and you will find that the majority of articles beg for increased productivity. In the journals we have been rebuked, chastised, put down by numbers recorded in competing nations. We have been pictured as clinging to punctured life rafts. Even though a rescue operation seemed to begin in the 1980s, we fear permanent damage to a workforce made to feel inferior, dehumanized, unskilled—productive units without faces. Employees became only units measured by dollars per hour.

The new division between the "haves" and "have nots" is no longer economic but raw power. The "haves" are those who manage and control; the "have nots" are the managed and controlled. Clarence B. Randall of Inland Steel fame wrote:

We have come to worship production as an end in itself, which, of course, it is not. It is precisely there that the honest critic of our way of life makes his attack and finds us vulnerable. Surely there must be for each person some ultimate value, some purpose, some mode of self-expression that makes the experience that we call life richer and deeper. To produce more and more with less and less effort is merely treading water unless we thereby release time and energy for the cultivation of the mind and the spirit and for those ends for which Providence placed us on earth.

I dare say we all like Mr. Randall's statement. But he wrote his book in 1952, and too few are like the Fleming Companies who have read it.

In 1958 William Hobgood, the assistant secretary of labor who mediated the 1978 coal strike, commented, "Historically labor has made most of its gains through confrontation, not cooperation, and historically, management has been most satisfied when it has employed pressure techniques." The associates concept seeks to change that.

Associates want to refute the statement of Greg Easterbrook when he said, "Industrial work is loud, monotonous, and tiring, and it nurtures in workers a deeply felt resentment of managers, who are imagined to be relaxing in wood-paneled luxury while the workers carry on the real jobs."

The most glaring downside of our merger mania is the secrecy dictated by the SEC to protect the stockholders. Because we cannot disclose impending matters we fail to lay the groundwork with the employees leaving them feeling like just another commodity to be worked out in the stock exchange—an utter disregard of human values and community welfare.

Yet I would do a disservice if I led you to believe associate means treating personnel by "whim and wish." Corporations are built on respected tradition, authority, and leadership. Obedience is inescapable. But the associate concept protects from corporate abuse. There must be structure if there is to be security.

When I was studying at the feet of Dr. C. Eugene Looper at Furman University, absorbing all I could from the head of the

Political Science Department, I never guessed the chapters he was still to write in his career. When I was a student, he held the distinction of being one of the youngest men to receive with honor his Ph.D. at Georgetown University, despite a service interruption. In his restless thirst for knowledge, he resigned from Furman to go to London and earn a second doctorate—this time in economics.

Dr. Looper came on the staff of Wachovia Bank to guide their economic forecasting. Wachovia was just beginning to accelerate statewide banking in North Carolina. But Wachovia's need for personnel was greater than that for forecasting. So Gene Looper, who is rather quiet and shy, was given that responsibility almost by default. What an excellent choice it turned out to be, for it is only the disciplined and emotionally controlled that can meet all the needs in any large company.

Only someone like an objective Gene Looper could spot the worth of a "country boy" like John Medlin, who today serves as CEO of First Wachovia Corporation. One of Gene's pet lines in teaching was, "It is the simple logic of great minds that baffles us." I have appended his basic personnel chart to illustrate his style.

Dick Williams of Fleming is not unlike Gene Looper, and it has been essential for Dick Harrison to have him beside him at corporate headquarters in Oklahoma City. Associate means burying the historic "carrot-stick" style of management. Corporate goals are unfulfilled unless they flow together with the personal goals of the associate. You can't fake it. It takes me back to this moment:

Linus to Charlie Brown: "You can't be a doctor. You don't love mankind."
Charlie Brown: "Mankind I love; it's just the people I can't stand!"

Putting the Associate Concept to Work

The associate concept depends on three factors: communication, hiring, and delegation.

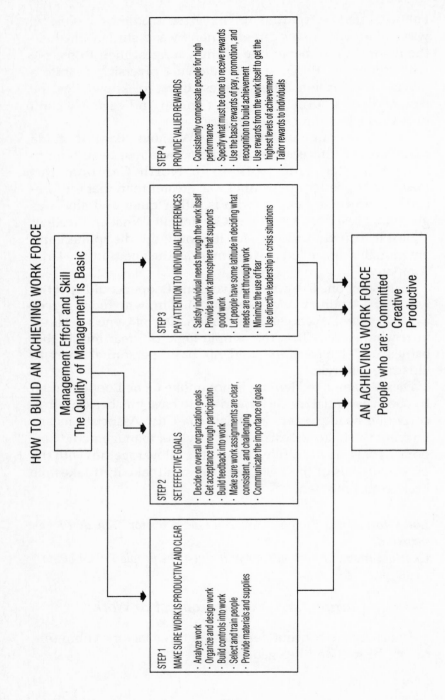

HOW TO BUILD AN ACHIEVING WORK FORCE

Management Effort and Skill
The Quality of Management is Basic

STEP 1
MAKE SURE WORK IS PRODUCTIVE AND CLEAR

· Analyze work
· Organize and design work
· Build controls into work
· Select and train people
· Provide materials and supplies

STEP 2
SET EFFECTIVE GOALS

· Decide on overall organization goals
· Get acceptance through participation
· Build feedback into work
· Make sure work assignments are clear, consistent, and challenging
· Communicate the importance of goals

STEP 3
PAY ATTENTION TO INDIVIDUAL DIFFERENCES

· Satisfy individual needs through the work itself
· Provide a work atmosphere that supports good work
· Let people have some latitude in deciding what needs are met through work
· Minimize the use of fear
· Use directive leadership in crisis situations

STEP 4
PROVIDE VALUED REWARDS

· Consistently compensate people for high performance
· Specify what must be done to receive rewards
· Use the basic rewards of pay, promotion, and recognition to build achievement
· Use rewards from the work itself to get the highest levels of achievement
· Tailor rewards to individuals

AN ACHIEVING WORK FORCE
People who are: Committed
Creative
Productive

Communication

In 1979 pollster Daniel Yankelovich found that 80 percent of all American workers believed they have a right to take part in decisions affecting their jobs. Eighty-eight percent of those between eighteen and twenty-five years of age felt this way. Tie this to a 1977 national worker survey (conducted by the University of Michigan for the Department of Labor) which revealed that the majority of American workers of all types did not receive enough information to do their jobs as well as they desired to do them.

"Scientific management" seems to have a built in noncommunication aspect. It eradicates emotion and intuition as being too unstable. Instead, a job is described in meticulous detail to match to the "exact" person. The work becomes a segmented task; the manager, a functional specialist who can quantify and qualify the task. Any interest in the person is avoided and rationalized as "getting too personal," or "an invasion of privacy" in our enlightened nonpaternal work world. The manager sees the employee as a human tool designed to make him look good. To those of such belief, associate is thought to be either hopelessly naive or, at best, window dressing.

Yankelovich's research records the shout of the people: "We're not a resource—we're people. We have much to contribute and in return we anticipate a quality of life. See me as someone with beliefs, attitudes, desires, and emotions."

We cannot approach the twenty-first century harboring the seventeenth-century error of René Descartes who saw the physical world as separate from the mind and the spirit. In practical terms, if we weigh people for their function and forget to include their feelings, they soon believe we put a disproportionate burden upon them for profit and progress.

What does associate communication include?

1. *Respect, which translates to participation by all involved.* There is a constant concern for individual dignity and worth. The treatment the customer receives ultimately hinges on how well the associates feel treated.

2. *Re-examination and resolution by all concerned to maintain compatibility between individual needs and corporate goals.* Grady

Gant, who built effective communications at Dixie Yarn Company of Chattanooga, stated Gant's Law of Human Relations: "People are *down* on what they are not *up* on and *in* on."

3. *Reinvestment in research and development for the future, as well as proper tools, equipment, and atmosphere in the present.* Relaxing on Australia's Gold Coast with Joe Gazel, I asked him how he had, just since 1956, built a manufacturing business supplying at least 80 percent of all underwear and sleepwear, in addition to 60 percent of all men's shirts? He told me he had the brightest, cleanest, most spacious factories in Australia (seeing one, I believe it). His employees knew they had the most modern equipment available in the world; that they had quality raw materials, bought competitively under what their competitors paid; that each plant engaged in research and constantly trained employees.

When I asked how he did this at the beginning, when he started on a shoestring, he told me that staying up to date and ahead is especially important when profits are lean, when "catch-up-ball" is unaffordable.

4. *Rewarding employees for diligent work.* In the next chapter, we will address executive rewards and awards, but here I am speaking of hourly or piece-goods associates. Again, Joe Gazel said never pay workers under their worth, even if you can. Employees must feel you have a conscience that matches theirs. Don't give them an excuse to "moonlight"; that divides their loyalty and energy. The job must be challenging by what is required as well as what is received.

5. *Rejecting any tendency to overlook fresh ideas.* 3M benefits from its rule of "refusing to discard any new ideas." Associate involvement soon becomes frustrated unless ideas are played back to the associates. Associate growth must be self-generated, but as with all growth, there must be a proper environment, feedback and response to fresh ideas. President Calvin Coolidge (who may have been "Silent Cal" in spoken word but he had a good pen) wrote: "Progress depends very largely on the encouragement of variety. Whatever tends to standardize the community *[or company]*, to establish fixed and rigid modes of thought, tends to fossilize society *[or my company]*. It is the ferment of ideas, the clash of disagreeing judgments, the privilege of the individual to develop his own thoughts,

and shape his own character, that makes progress possible."
(*Emphasis added.*)

Hiring

In hiring, the benefit of the associate approach is even
clearer. The very terminology is helpful. When I realize I will
be calling the "new hire" my "associate," it prevents either
callousness at the point of employing or casual treatment early
on the job. We know the treatment of an associate in the first
days on the job often determines just how many days the
individual stays on as an associate.

Parenthetically, I suggest a fundamental question, "Do we
need to fill the vacancy?" Overemployment, which leads to
underuse of abilities, is cruel. Every vacancy should be tested.
Can the position be divided among existing associates, giving
them greater sense of worth and an avenue to salary increase?
It was ironic that the year textile interests took the lead in
pressuring President Reagan to curb offshore products was
also the record year for textile profits. But hundreds of jobs
lost were not regained. The textile companies learned how to
be leaner and meaner, thus giving greater significance to each
worker's contribution. They also installed the automation that
they had resisted. Then, as always, tough times clean from
the marketplace some companies that should have been eliminated years before.

When a vacancy is substantiated or growth begs for more
associates, then what is the profile of people you will embrace
as "associates"? Much more personal than just recruiting a
worker, the Associate Concept—although it recognizes vari-
ances in talent and responsibility—also accepts the premise
that no position can be thought menial nor feared as mighty.
This is not democratizing the associate but a recognition that,
although talents vary, individual worth does not.

Some years ago a consortium of steel companies in Pittsburgh asked me to assist their personnel people in hiring
procedures. A mature industry seeking a new generation of
employees, they felt my constant campus and military speaking gave me valuable insights.

So I designed for my lecture and subsequent discussion

three questions that would give the directions I felt essential. It was an effort to cure the disease of "Hire in haste; repent in leisure." Being introduced to the associate involvement by Dick Harrison only solidifies my convictions about careful hiring.

The three questions were:

1. *Why are you seeking employment here?*

Is it because a member of your family or close friend is already working here? Is that person totally satisfied, or did you hear we're expanding and you need a job, any job?

I believe an *entrance interview* at your company should include an *exit review* from their previous work. Appropriate questions might include:

> a) Why did you leave, or are you willing to leave, your present employment?
> b) What were your direct duties? Did your abilities comfortably match your duties? Did you feel overemployed or underemployed?
> c) What was your proudest moment on the previous job?
> d) What do you consider the greatest strength you bring to us?
> e) What was the most irritating aspect of your last job?
> f) What was your opinion of the people working most closely with you? (Remember, you're going to make him an "associate," that intimate.)
> g) Did you have a favorite supervisor and why? (Supervisors, in most instances, are mirrors.)

2. *How interested are you in this job?*

Is this job a way station until you get the one you really want? Is this part of your preparation or learning experience? Is this the job to keep body clothed and fed until you find your niche?

You'll phrase the questions more indirectly, but you will weigh what you get. Temporary people or even part-time employees are essential in some companies like the airlines or local supermarkets. Also, many a valued associate originally came to work for a short time but found a career.

You really want to determine how much you can afford to

invest in the person in fairness to your other associates. You seek to determine whether the applicant is transitory or permanent and also whether he seeks a career ladder or is happy working at just about entry level.

3. *How can I help you succeed in your position?*

Remember I had prepared this approach for the managers of a state-of-the-art industry. This third question raised some eyebrows, cleared some throats, and caused some groans and grunts.

It was time to remind them that *manage* and *manipulate* come from the same Latin root word. Jesus was not trying to humble the leader as much as give him and us the best psychological advice available when he said: "He that would be great, must serve." In education we say that if a large number of students flunk, it doesn't indicate a strong teacher using sound discipline but an ineffective teacher, poorly enlisting support in the learning process. The same can be applied to industry.

My point is that being an associate imposes upon the leader the responsibility to share in the feelings as well as the intelligence of fellow associates. Simply put, the associate's effectiveness depends upon those with whom he is associated.

One of today's problems, although we're reluctant to admit it, is that the business leadership generation now in control considers itself the last hardworking generation—the last of the great Americans because we experienced the Great Depression and World War II. At the private club, the eavesdropper would get the impression that we are the last defenders of the private enterprise system, the keepers of the flame, and the discerners of the truth. It is somewhat difficult to be an associate when one side is so prejudiced. How wrong we are in the light of the sterling contributions of those who are carelessly called Yuppies.

Associate has "mentoring" built in. Mentoring is a two-way street. It is not just saying, "I want to learn from you." It is also reaching out a hand or, better still, putting an arm around someone. Nowhere else in contemporary society does the privilege of helping come as directly as in the corporation. To exercise the associate option, one must be subtle and sensitive, fusing aggression and affection.

There are always disappointments when we deal with each other, but the goal is to perfect a hiring policy that will avoid the shoals downstream. And there are problems. A recent survey revealed that forty percent of a corporation's employees did not believe that their complaints had been handled properly by their supervisor. Let's not naively bet the company store on a printed survey. Too much depends on the way the questions are asked. Yet there is too much here to ignore.

DELEGATION: NOT A CHORE BUT AN EXCITING CHOICE

The final ingredient of the associates approach is delegation.

1. Delegation Is Not Autocratic

Delegation is not passing out favors or patting the top of the head. How can people feel like associates if all authority and power are held by one person, even two or three? If leadership means holding tight reins while wearing filed spurs, then the term associate is an insult!

One of the first questions I ask corporations seeking my services is, "How is responsibility shared?" The answer provides my quickest insight into the company.

Sure, the buck finally rests on a single desk, but growth comes by multiplying oneself.

Think of it. Jesus Christ promised the disciples that as great as His achievements were, they would do greater work than He (John 14:12). Was He suggesting that they had His stature and deity? Of course not. He was underlining the principle that is found in a Spanish proverb: "Three men helping one another will do as much as six singly."

Delegation answers at least three questions.

• *Do I have enough self-confidence to trust my judgment?* Delega-

120

tion has little to do with the trustworthiness of my associates, but it does measure my self-trust.

• *How do I appraise myself?* Do I recognize my strengths and accept my limitations, realizing the company would be injured if I didn't delegate? The nondelegater is often like the king saying to his groomsman: "I look out the window and I don't see any hunger, any suffering, any deprivation. Why are the people congregating, unruly and shouting?"

The aide, finally screwing up his courage, replies, "Sire, it's because you're not looking out a window but into a mirror."

My observation is that one who is not delegating designates himself Charles Atlas and sees ninety-nine-pound weaklings around him. The more driven he is to rule, often the more generously he pays his colleagues to sit around him for cosmetic affect.

• *What is my vision for the company?* How far can I see? Am I asking the people out there nearer the scene to use their eyes as well?

Delegation, which is a chore for some, has been an exciting choice for me. My two brothers were only sixteen months apart, which almost assures sibling rivalry. There was a gap before I came along. Although on occasion I viewed them with consternation, most times they were my heroes. They, I felt, were more talented than I. Anytime I was with them, I felt my image enhanced. That didn't take away the feeling that there were some things I could do better than either of them; but at an early age, it seems I concluded subconsciously that I could get more done efficiently through others. Dad reminds me that at age ten I organized the mowing of the parsonage lawns so each kid helping felt rewarded as a contributor. (Instead of admiring my plan, Dad thought I might be listening too often to the *Amos 'n Andy* radio show and emulating the Kingfish.)

Delegation is not autocratic but asking.

2. Delegation Is Not Assignment

There is a difference between delegation and redistribution. Some people have everything funneled to their office so they can figure who can do it best; to them leadership is passing out assignments. This is just redistribution.

Delegation is the conviction that you are associated with people who not only can do the job but will also actually do it better than you could.

It is their field of expertise. Now, expertise is a key. It's more than unloading the nitty gritty. One of President Jimmy Carter's glaring weaknesses was surrounding himself on the White House staff with inexperienced errand boys without competence to accept shared responsibility. Their ineptness became the administration's ineffectiveness.

Turning to capable associates not only causes them to grow but increases their confidence in you.

John David of Sydney leads, by far, the largest wholesale food corporation in Australia with annual sales exceeding $2.2 billion. His style is to meet with key executives and first see if they agree with his outline of the challenge before them. After he is assured they share a common focus, he asks simple but penetrating questions:

"This is a substantial project. Is it too ambitious for us?"

"Is there any way we, with our limited staff and resources, can seize this opportunity?"

These are not patronizing questions, but a revelation of John's will, seasoned with doubts and needing his associates' reassurance and resolution.

When I accepted the "herculean task" of scouting's restoration, my first decision was choosing someone totally trustworthy and with exceptional capabilities but, at that moment, underutilized. His name: Frank Parachini. His mind was a bear trap. He was tough, having accepted some of scouting's roughest assignments, but unrecognized. He wasn't colorful, but he was determined. When the history of scouting's revival is written, I doubt if Frank's name will even appear; but I assure you it is written on God's record. I told him we would get along well: "We're so much alike. Frank, you're in your sixties; I'm in my forties. You're a devout Catholic still enjoying Latin masses while I'm Southern Baptist. You're Italian; my dad is Syrian/Lebanese. You're politically a liberal Democrat; I come from the Robert Taft side of Republicans. Frank, we're just like two peas in a pod!" (The last thing a leader needs is clones.) While I think the exception proves the rule, Frank felt each exception weakens the rule. Frank was my total opposite.

With Frank at my side, we choose equally capable specialists, such as Curt Wessner in employee relations; Bart Nourse in employee training; Ernie Cuccaro in employee benefits. Then we practiced my leadership style of "controlled confrontation":

Disruption and doubts are introduced to force a thorough examination of goals and practices. While outside the door it might have sounded as if the fur was flying, inside the door, feathers were ruffled just enough to reveal the full wingspan.

Central to my leadership style is my belief that recognition without responsibility causes resentment. Edwin Bliss summed it up well: "The key to delegation is the word entrust. When you delegate, you entrust the entire matter to the other person, along with sufficient authority to make necessary decisions. This is quite a different thing from saying, 'Just do what I tell you to do.'"

3. Delegation Is Not Abdication

Delegation is not handing the ball off and it is not throwing the lead block. Instead, the leader defines what he does best while supporting his associates, refining what they can do in concert. Each year I choose a motto for the flyleaf of my pocket datebook. In 1974 I wrote:

"I do not want to spend 1974 doing that which someone else does better while I can do something no one else does as well."

This was not ego talking. It was accepting the fact that each of us is an exclusive creation of God endowed with complementary but diverse talents.

Jack Campbell is the leader who moved the manufacturing

home of high-quality upholstered furniture from Grand Rapids, Michigan, to High Point, North Carolina, back in the years when the South had limited, moderate furniture-making capacity and an abnormal amount of borax. The bastion of quality was "up North." Recognized decorators looked at the South with disdain. Yet the post-war boom demanded expansion of manufacturing facilities to an area with a ready, non-unionized labor pool. When Jack decided to bring the highly prized Schoonbeck furniture line to High Point, he knew the announcement was met with disbelief, derision, and— cruelest of all—refusal to buy.

So Jack prepared for the 1954 market. The buyers came in droves to purchase Schoonbeck made in Grand Rapids and they bought heavily. Only after he had the firm orders did Jack identify the pieces built not in Grand Rapids but in High Point, giving the buyers the privilege of canceling the order. Very few exercised the option.

The "rest of the story . . . ," as Paul Harvey could report, is that Schoonbeck started its successful odyssey manufacturing the finest furniture short of handmade with its total operation moved to North Carolina and complementing its fashionable upholstery by merging with Henredon case goods. Little wonder MASCO made it the crown jewel in its aggressive acquisition thrust of 1986.

Delegation made the rapid growth possible. Jack is extremely sensitive to people. He promised furniture that would last as long as the customer possesses it, and he hunted for a proficient production superintendent, a creative chief designer, an astute material purchaser, an enlightened chief decorator, and an excitable sales director. But if delegation is not abdication, what does the leader choose to retain as his main strength?

Just as challenging as delegation is recognizing what must be kept so that the culture of the company is not injured.

As an example, Jack felt he could make two major contributions. He would surround himself with creative, "pride of authorship," sensitive artists and meld them into a team complementing each other. He found that such creative people responded to casual rather than structured staff meetings. Important agenda items did not wait for a set time. Responsiveness and on-time delivery became part of Schoonbeck's profile. A company can't be slow internally and punctual externally.

Jack didn't publish staff meeting agendas lest each person become preoccupied with his portion and not lend his mind to the overviews. Understanding the sensitive psyches of artists, Jack used the creative questions to produce input. Asking the question implied he would "buy into" the answer. He praised his staff for their accepted creative renderings and accepted responsibility for items the public rejected.

This reminds me of William Boetcker's appraisal: "The man who is worthy of being a leader will never complain about the stupidity of his helpers, the ingratitude of mankind, or the inappreciation of the public. They are all part of the game of life. To meet them and not overcome them and not go down before them in disgust, discouragement or defeat, that is the final proof of power."

The other responsibility Jack didn't delegate was lending his imagination to sophisticated and subtle fabric selection. A Schoonbeck fabric glows alone in a crowd. He encouraged his team not only to utilize the premier fabrics from Clarence House Imports or F. Schumacker or Greff where they received pattern exclusivity, but also to be brazen enough to buy "sunburst" fabrics from an artist loft, or from a company that could even be out of business before reorder time. Can you beat matching quality with serendipity?

Jack Campbell illustrates delegation without abdication. He knows better than to delegate to the point of giving away his natural strengths.

One last thought on delegation. As you move toward making your executive team feel like full associates, be sure to acquire an effective executive secretary. Actually, I don't think you can get any corporation in order unless your own office sets the example.

For eighteen years Mary Helen Batten has walked step by step with me. During my twenty-seven months in the scouting project, she coordinated things between our home office in High Point and the national office in scouting; and it was also during this period that I became chairman of IGA.

Today Mary Helen still amazes me as she balances my schedule between IGA responsibilities, Eastern Air Lines, corporate board meetings, our foundation and scholarship program, and all of my speaking. We have walked through the best of times and the worst of times, through family sorrows and family joys. Yet I doubt if anyone ever calling the office felt that Mary Helen was having a "down" day or felt in any way that she was annoyed by the call. Over and over again, I hear, "We sure enjoy the relationship we have built with Mary Helen. You're blessed with an efficient office."

Not a day passes that my wife, Buren, and I don't thank God for our association with Mary Helen. Not only does she know the mechanics of her job, but more importantly, she knows how and when to pick me up when I am down . . . when to pull me down a bit when I am too high. It's certainly not patronizing in our case but reality when we say, "Mary Helen is family."

Using the associates concept is not a procedure alone. It is a conviction. Dick Harrison, reflecting on his earlier experiences of life, consciously developed a leadership style built on his belief that efficient productivity is the natural performance of pleased people. The last chapter shows how Roger Milliken, believing that a company's sterling asset is people, literally moved in with them so he could look out through their eyes; and in the next chapter we'll see another leader "keep on keeping on" with high intensity when he is emphatically reinforced.

So, we've seen that if the leader is comfortable enough with himself to have associates, he starts with the executive team and then moves to upside-down management. However, hourly paid employees can not feel like associates unless they sense that the officers who occupy the executive suite are a team of associates. The executive associates exemplify by word and deed that they courageously move forward because they have full confidence in their associates on the firing line throughout the company. The fellow riding shotgun is of the same value as the fellow perched up on the seat and called wagon master.

Labor difficulties, uneven economic conditions, and political uncertainties—not only do they not destroy the associate approach, but they actually strengthen it. No company has had to face a tougher labor climate than Bozzuto's of Cheshire, Connecticut. Yet well do I remember the cold winter day when I enjoyed with all the employees, from the floor sweeper to the chairman, a warm and marvelous Italian meal, not in a restaurant but right out on the shipping dock of the warehouse. It was like sitting down around the campfire, bonded together in the breaking of bread. We were associates.

8

Takin' Up the Slack

The high-water mark of western migration occurred in 1850 when 55,000 pilgrims left the United States at Kansas City to seek the promised land in Oregon.

In the early 1840s, wagon trains of twenty to thirty wagons could negotiate the plains without much organization, but when the trains grew to fifty and sixty wagons, the wagon masters had to come up with some new methods of safety and control.

So the trains were split into segments of five wagons each. The members of those parties left in the morning together; shared lunch and evening meal together; helped each other with ox and wagon problems; cheered and comforted each other at their own campfires. So the line of wagons would be five wagons, then a gap, then five more wagons and a gap, and so on.

As evening drew near, the wagon master would send his pilot forward on horseback to scout out a suitable plain where all of the segments would rejoin in one huge circle. So proficient were these pilots in marking out the needed diameter of their circle that the last wagon neatly closed the loop without any wagon in the circle before them having to move.

After the oxen were unhitched they could be left in the circle or led to another guarded area. The tongue of each wagon was inserted into the rear axle assembly of the one before it and secured there by chains. Guards were then posted around the perimeter. So formidable was this tactic that no Indian war party ever attacked any western travelers employing it.

What the wagon master really worried about were the straggler wagons, those that because of breakdown or illness had to pull out of the segment and drift in when they could. These were the ones that were vulnerable to Indian raids and injury.

Physical strength and mental ingenuity were needed to cajole, encourage, help, and rebuild—to get the troubled wagon back to the safety of the train.

The Great Leader Guides Different People in Pursuit of a Common Goal

We have become accustomed to painting our leaders somewhat larger than life—way out in front of their corporations—dragging the corporate team forward by the sheer magnetism of personality. The leader is seen as the dominating suitor overwhelming the reluctant damsel. Such ego drive may for a short time be mistaken as leadership, but it evaporates in the first crisis.

The leader exerts special influence over a number of people for their mutual benefit. His personality in action molds the group together. His leadership traits are authenticated by the group's willing followership. In most instances, misunderstood leaders are not ahead of their time as much as they have separated themselves from their time. Conceptual thinking, creative genius, and expansive vision may mark their individualities, but progress depends on complementing those talents with an empathy that seeks to understand one's followers, sense their needs, and suggest ways that both the leader and the follower can be satisfied with the end result.

Leadership, as we have seen in people like Roger Milliken and Dick Harrison, is mental contact leading to a social process that subdues dominance and heightens delegation. An attitude of "give and take" transforms a dissatisfying job to a satisfying mission.

The person who views himself as a hero in his own time feels "center stage" is his due. Such self-anointed leaders, rising on the shoulders of their own press releases, are actually indifferent, narrow, fickle, duplicitous, cowardly, stubborn, and isolated. They attempt to overcompensate, lest they be found out for what they are. My selected leaders have praise, vitality, enthusiasm, positiveness, friendliness, trustworthiness, and sympathy.

So in each chapter I have taken a bifocal approach to leadership. The emphasis on the leader is matched by the effect on the led.

To be sure, raw survival may cause the autocratic, personality-cult leader to have a following. There is a lot of truth in the perversion of the Golden Rule to "He who has the gold, sets the rules." With calculated smiles and measured pleasantness, the personality-cult leader charms his way; but gradually his failure to build an infrastructure reveals to his followers that he succeeds at their expense. No hatred is as severe as when love is followed blindly, only to find the so-called leader absent when the dead end is reached. The extreme was cited by Emil Ludwig in his biography, *Napoleon*: "But the crowd must be learning to hate him; for, in that darkling hour, hundreds of unarmed citizens, idle spectators, women have perished. What is that to him? It is not his aim to be loved."

Even if the autocratic personality-cult leader is warm and paternalistic, he is unveiled as cruel if he has not developed individual initiative in his followers. Wanting to be all things to all people, he may well leave them nothing. This leader fails to let people loose and encourage their development so they might take his place and even overshadow him. No matter how kind, he flunks the test of serving his followers.

The wagon master earned respect and control by understanding that stimulation and energy derive from guiding different people in pursuit of a common goal.

The Leaders of a Worldwide Success Story—Coca-Cola

Such a twentieth-century wagon master resides at the world headquarters of Coca-Cola in Atlanta, Georgia. Yes, I mean *world* headquarters! How do you keep the wagons together when they reach into over 150 countries of the world? It is one thing to leave your office and wander through an adjacent plant or store, quite a different thing when the employees circle the world—with different cultures and different tongues sharing the same truth, integrity, value, character, consistency, clarity, confidence, pride, and purpose. All of this energy is directed toward selling people 250 million times a day to add a simple moment of pleasure—"the Pause that Refreshes"—to their often prosaic daily lives. Such a cajoling and complimenting leader is Donald R. Keough, president and chief operating officer of The Coca-Cola Company.

Few would question that Roberto C. Goizueta, chairman and CEO, has one of the fine-tuned conceptual minds of world business. The Cuban-born, U.S.-educated executive had built-in excuses to be mediocre at worst and timid at best but, instead, has honored the legacy of the late Robert Woodruff by believing simple refreshment can stimulate otherwise drab moments, whether it be a Coke, a glass of OJ, a cup of coffee, or a movie. Handpicked by Mr. Woodruff in 1980, Goizueta changed Coke from the starchiness of his predecessor to " . . . an enthusiasm akin to that of schoolboys released from a long detention period."

Up to his recent retirement, Lebanese-born but Egyptian-raised, Sam Ayoub was chief financial officer and the steward of Coca-Cola's abnormally large resources. In fact, Coke had such an international flavor in its executives—including Brian Dyson from Argentina and Tony Amon from Middle Europe—that Roberto Goizueta had a belly laugh at a Los Angeles analysis meeting when Don Keough, following him and Sam Ayoub to the podium, opened his remarks in his perfect Midwestern diction: "At the outside I'd like to apologize for my accent. I hope it doesn't detract from the international flavor of the company."

Coca-Cola had its territory staked out. It possessed the most recognized English label in the world from its colloquial world headquarters in Atlanta, Georgia. But new frontiers remain the dream of its leadership.

Yes, a few years ago Coke was lulled to sleep, tranquilized by its own successes and excesses; but its main rival Pepsi forgot the old legend that says if you finally get a giant to nap, be sure to tiptoe around him. Enter the Goizueta era, turning the operational reins over to Don Keough. If Coke was blinking, as a somewhat suspect author suggests, it was the reaction of looking into the brilliant light of its 100th birthday cake that celebrated its record-setting year.

Don Keough looks the part of a wagon master. Nebraska-born, rising through the experiences of each aspect of the company, Don possesses a robust Irish wit; is devoted to church and family; is chairman of trustees at Notre Dame University; is quick to laugh and instinctively gregarious; is firm but friendly. He has innate sound judgment. Former Omaha Mayor Bob Cunningham, a Creighton classmate of Don's, described him like this: "He's a big, warm teddy bear type of Irishman, a very funny man."

Don Keough is the personification of the United Technologies advertisement editorial in *The Wall Street Journal*:

> Let's get rid of management.
> People don't want to be managed.
> They want to be led.
> Whoever heard of a world manager? World leader, yes.
> Educational leader. Political leader. Religious leader.
> Scout leader. Community leader. Labor leader. Business leader. They lead.
> They don't manage . . . if you want to manage somebody, manage yourself.
> Do that well, and you will be ready to stop managing,
> And start leading.

This may have been on Teddy Roosevelt's mind when he wrote: "People ask the difference between a leader and a boss. The leader works in the open, the boss in the covert. The leader leads, the boss drives."

Don Keough is the consummate leader possessed by the ultimate virtue—great loves. If love doesn't carry a man beyond himself, it is not love. Love that is always discreet, always wise, always sensible and calculating, never reaching beyond itself, is synthetic. Love makes the leader magnetically vulnerable. Of course, I'm not writing of weakness but strength. Love without courage and wisdom is mere sentimentality. Strength without love usually becomes egotism that leads to suspicion, distrust, and jealousy. Such strength tends to take the form of grandiose ideas and overestimation of one's power and control, giving a false sense of omnipotence.

Leadership built on devotion cannot be passive. We can expect to get action from Don. He defies the observation of Paul Vilandre of Convergent Technologies who marveled, "Smokestack industry gets hung up on the elegance of the decision vs. the substance" (*The Wall Street Journal*, Jan. 10, 1985). Don is willing to be assertive but realistic enough to encourage assertiveness from others and humble enough to acknowledge the superiority of ideas presented by others. *The effort is not to make people feel that they are of use to Coca-Cola but that they are of value to Coca-Cola.*

Picture with me a significant gathering of Don's associates. Here their president is preparing to speak. You can imagine an international executive standing behind a lectern reading in *ex cathedra* tones the address carefully homogenized by his writers. Not Don Keough! He speaks informally from his heart and with a touch of humor on winning. He tells his audience he can recognize a winner once a gold medal is hung around his neck or the profits of the corporation have skyrocketed or a new product has been successfully introduced. "Winners," he has said, "come in every size and shape; they are introverts and extroverts. They are educated, uneducated; some of them are charismatic and articulate, and others are dull as dishwater."

He then refers to a sociology professor from one of the country's major universities who spent his life studying leadership by tracing the careers of five thousand former students: "I have come to the conclusion that the only way one can determine a leader is to look at the person and see if anybody is following him."

After democratizing the audiences with such comments, Don Keough then stimulates them upward by sharing "Keough's Commandments for Losing":

1. Quit taking risks.
2. Be content.
3. Before you make any move, always ask yourself, "What will my investors think?"
4. Avoid change.

5. Be totally inflexible—stay on the course, no matter what.

6. Rely totally on research and experts to make decisions for you.

7. Be more concerned with status than service.

8. Concentrate on your competitor instead of your customer.

9. Put yourself first in everything you do, ahead of your customers and suppliers.

10. Memorize the formula "TGE . . . That's Good Enough" to set a ceiling on quality.

Then add a bonus rule:

11. Find a way to rationalize the slowing of growth.

Go back and read these eleven "Commandments for Losing" and again see yourself sitting in the sizable audience of Coca-Cola peers. Even without knowing Don Keough, you can see the smile with which each point was developed and the compliment implied therein. Absent are the placating empty words designed to be warm but cold when spoken by a president either wanting to be quoted correctly by the press or fearing being quoted at all. Don is actually complimenting his associates' abilities. He knows that none of them would knowingly do these things, though any of us can get careless. What he is really doing is praising the group into constructive performance.

There is nothing new about his approach really, for it was verbalized by Dr. Elton Mayo of Harvard Graduate School of Business Administration. The testing ground was the Hawthorne Plant of Western Electric in suburban Chicago. The testing time was 1927-1932. The theory that Dr. Mayo proved was that workers tend to cluster together into informal groups in order to fill a void in their lives. *The void is a person's need for companionship and cooperation.* The Industrial Revolution depersonalized man. If that was true in 1930, think about our automated age now beginning to utilize robotic technology. At least in 1930 the worker might be reinforced at home while, today, fewer than 25 percent of our homes are traditional, meaning both parents in the home.

So Dr. Mayo's prescription was to cultivate communication between employer and employee and to put supervision in the hands of people to whom respect for other persons came naturally. Supervisors were to be trained in the skills of listening, understanding, and eliciting cooperation which was quite a departure from the image of the straw boss of that day. Dr. Mayo literally became an industrial evangelist. He had a simple message: Productivity declines when work deteriorates into an impersonal exchange of money for labor. He called it *Anomie,* which left workers feeling rootless, unimportant, and confused by the indifference to their environment. The only other place I have seen this word used was in James Michener's novel *Texas* when the settlers were lost in the expanse. If people became docile, they didn't have to be angry; they just became woeful, inefficient producers. The Siamese twins of productivity and quality died simultaneously.

Now let's bring Dr. Mayo and Don Keough together in these last years of the twentieth century and join them with Daniel Webster who defined labor as, "One of the great elements of society . . . the great substantial interest on which we all stand. No feudal service or the irksome drudgery of one race subjected to another but labor . . . intelligent, manly, independent, thinking and acting for one's self, earning one's own wages, educating childhood, maintaining worship, claiming the right to the elective franchise and helping to uphold the great fabric of the state. That is labor, and all my sympathies are with it."

Dr. Mayo has said it and Don Keough is shouting, "Amen." People work effectively where people feel warm. Can you imagine a simpler word than warm? Yet isn't that true? Where we feel a sense of belonging and a sense of worth, we respond productively. We need that sense of achievement, self-esteem, recognition, and security even more than we need the money, for as the University of Michigan found in a 1977 study, three out of four Americans would prefer to be working even if they could live comfortably without working for the rest of their lives. This desire to make people feel "warm" worked for Dr. Mayo a half century ago and works for Don Keough today.

Don said on an occasion, "I have a calling card. It says, 'Donald R. Keough, President of The Coca-Cola Company.' Now in the last analysis, the only thing that is really mine is the 'Donald R. Keough.' I am a temporary president. I am a

temporary resident of this fancy office. I hope that when I
have to tear that card up and when I carry one that says just,
'Donald R. Keough,' I will be enough of a total person that I
will be considered worthwhile. I think about that . . . a lot."

How does this attitude translate into actuality with Don
Keough's corporate team? Ask him: "A lot of managers focus
on weaknesses. And we all have them. I think that is a fundamental mistake. You have to look at the beauty spots. We all
have those, too. When you do that, and let the person sense it,
then you get all the best that's in them. And they are not
demeaned or destroyed by your constantly reaching in to find
their weaknesses."

*When you make people feel good about themselves, you are helping
them say, "God, you didn't waste your creative power on me."*

What does Don mean by "beauty spots"? It's the climate he
has created. Whether in Houston or Singapore, his call begins: "You have to be proud of increased sales in Classic Coke.
The public sure shouted their loyalty when we introduced our
new formula, and I'm proud we could respond so quickly.
Now I notice you still have that nagging problem with your
division. What's your game plan? You do feel it's solvable?
Well, here's the best thinking from our end. Are we a help to
you, and how can we better assist you?"

The entire tone promotes a successful conclusion with the
person nearest the problem receiving the credit. The tone is
neither false praise nor destructive flattery. Victor Frankl, the
veteran of the Holocaust, a psychologist and teacher, taught
us in *Man's Search for Meaning* that unreal optimism can be
more damaging than criticism or pessimism. By comparison,
candor can be upbeat.

Don Keough joins other admired leaders in addressing
issues with the attitude of helping, not condemning. Explora-
tory surgery is an act of desperation. You desire to cut in with
the idea of where you'll come out. I hear you talking back to
me as you read these pages: "Tom, business is hard and harsh;
you can't always be pleasant." Wrong! You can be pleasant.
The more pleasant you are, the firmer you can be. Pleasantness helps you to look without apology for the silver lining

of each cloud. You look for opportunity to celebrate. You hope, *by praise,* to turn any little progress into momentum.

Again you talk back: "Whenever I'm critical, it is constructive criticism." Constructive criticism is never identified by the mouth speaking, but by the ears listening. Praise is the rite of passage that allows you to be constructively helpful. Going through the heartaches of scouting, as well as the repositioning of IGA, I have found I can face the tough decisions and still be pleasant. Pleasantness may test whether you are rightfully objective or wrongly subjective.

Leadership is not being nice to people. Leadership is recognizing that people need an environment where they can be nice to themselves.

In each of us are sterling strengths and woeful weaknesses. The leader's role is to create the atmosphere where the person's strengths outweigh his weaknesses. It's much like the missionary asking a recent convert how he was enjoying his newfound faith. The convert quietly replied, "Ah, Mr. Missionary, I find I have within me two dogs. I have a good dog and I have a bad dog. They're always fighting."

"And which dog wins?" queried the missionary.

"That's easy," replied the convert, "whichever one I say 'Sic 'em' to."

Leadership is warmly encouraging your associates to whisper, "Sic 'em," to their strengths. To put it another way, when you help associates to appreciate expressed appreciation, you're watching them move in the right direction.

Refining Your Employee Appraisal System

Employees properly expect reassurance. A worldwide corporation sets the example for each of its facilities by keeping an open-door policy at the corporate headquarters. Communication is every leader's responsibility. Pruning the grapevines that strangle best intentions is a necessity. Don Keough makes a practice of meeting new Coke people wherever he travels and is blessed with an incredibly retentive mind for names and faces. He is aware that even the international success of

Coca-Cola doesn't erase the twin questions that have a way of popping up: How sound is our business in the face of our competition? How secure is my job?

Here's where an effective appraisal system should be "a given." One of my first corporate responsibilities was to review the organization's appraisal system. "Appraisal" has never been an attractive word to me. It presumes a role that makes me uncomfortable. *Random House Dictionary* defines appraisal as "the act of estimating the value of an asset. . . ." We agree our greatest asset is "people," but calling them assets is dehumanizing. The appraiser who views himself as an amateur psychologist compounds this problem. A chill sweeps over me when I hear appraisers use "buzz words" to classify employees. They adopt that nagging tendency to solve a new problem by giving it a new name!

With the responsibility to perfect the appraisal system, I studied ten corporations, beginning at the Pentagon with the highly structured system of the U.S. Air Force and ending at Hughes Aircraft where my late brother Ted was senior scientist.

Not one of the ten was satisfied with the way they appraised. That was encouraging! Any time we are satisfied with our judgmental procedures toward our fellowman, we are in trouble. We should always be refining our efforts to be fairer and more insightful. Also, most appraisals are downward or, at best parallel, but never upward. Those who report to us seldom, if ever, have the opportunity to appraise us. One of the many reasons I admire Colonel Frank Borman was his decision to encourage a team of union and nonunion employees to run a report card on him. It was a team effort so no subordinates would feel threatened. Frank felt that because they owned 25 percent of the nonnegotiable stock and couldn't sell if dissatisfied like public investors, they should be able to appraise him to help the Eastern Air Lines.

I reached several conclusions about appraisals.

1. *Even if the form is structured, the actual appraisal should be done in an informal setting.* Don't even begin unless you have time and hope to be free from interruptions. Never should the two people be across a desk from each other. A desk lends

itself to an adversarial relationship. I usually sit beside the person, possibly making a few informal notes, and then filling out the necessary form later. After filling out the form and writing a summary essay, I sit with the person again to go over my observations. Hopefully, he or she will be comfortable signing off on it.

2. *My goal is to dwell more on the future opportunities than on the past performance.*

3. *My desire is to lead the person to self-appraisal, giving me the privilege to be the listener and catalyst.* Whenever people are free to set their own standards, they are more stringent on themselves than you would have been on them. Leaders in effective corporations gladly grant employees more rights than the average company, but the employees are challenged to accept greater responsibilities enthusiastically. The proper balance of rights and responsibilities equals effectiveness.

Rights don't democratize the corporation but underscore caring leadership. People want leaders to lead—make no mistake about it.

Everyone Needs A Leader

In January of 1986 I sat at Food Marketing Institute's Mid-Year Convention listening to Professor D. Quinn Mills of Harvard University. Although I respect him, I found myself shaking my head negatively. Though it seemed out of character, I felt Dr. Mills was bordering on insulting his audience. He was using People Express Airline to teach us the "new wave of corporate climate." First, I felt it was a poor choice to hype any company that had been in existence less than a half dozen years. Continuity is a basic factor in leadership. Secondly, Dr. Mills was making the case for a democratic workplace where the officers sold tickets and pilots loaded luggage. Thank goodness flight attendants didn't fly planes!

From the first year of operation, I had predicted the demise of People Express. How people like Dr. Mills could get "carried away" I'll never understand. People want a hierarchy; otherwise, they feel insecure about privileges. As Dr. Mayo had found, people tend to cluster and, not given leadership, will designate their own. People Express is now history, and the only people more embarrassed than the creditors are the professors.

There is no question who leads Coca-Cola. In the uncertain moments before they turned Classic Coke into a bonanza guaranteeing more shelf space in the food store, Robert Goizueta and Don Keough, not a surrogate, met the press and bit the bullet. People rally around people, not philosophy.

With all the opportunities at Coca-Cola, lifetime employment is not a consideration. They don't roll heads carelessly nor move people indiscriminately, but they also won't allow good employees to be undermined nor the company to become hostage to bungling.

Coke had gone through a period before the Goizueta-Keough era where all of us in the business community were hearing their squeaky revolving door too often. Don Keough puts determination far ahead of termination unless behavior is flagrant. He challenges his personnel people to work diligently to place the right person in the right job.

Good people can be lost through misplacement, especially when the company stretches around the world. I am old enough to remember that Jimmy Tabor flunked out as a pitcher but became a star third baseman with the Boston Red Sox in an infield that included York, Doerr, Pesky, and Tebbetts. I recall that Bob Lemon couldn't hit his weight as a centerfielder but led the Cleveland Indians into the World Series as an All-Star pitcher. As someone who has had to do more than his quota of firing, I believe firing is as important a role as hiring and is necessary for a healthy corporation, but each instance must be tested and justified.

A bottom line is operative in this chapter. The pilgrims and the wagon master were pushing together for the reward of a promised land. The pragmatic side of your praising and cajoling in a corporation is the financial reward. A worldwide corporation like Coke has to have salary management but flexibility to make exceptions. The exceptions actually legitimize the rules. You can be rewarded with more than normal increments and you can merit jumping several positions. For years I have quarreled with surveys that place salary somewhere between fifth and sixth of the ten things a person wants from a job. Not for a minute do I believe there are many people who will say, "Just pay me enough and I'm your boy." At the same time, most people probably value salary second or third, but in a false search for nobility, they feel it crass to put it there. Anticipating good returns for your efforts is proper.

Motivating People the W. H. Belk Way

One man who had native sense about people was the late William Henry Belk, one of the unsung geniuses of the Southeast. The four-hundred-store company that bears his name is one hundred years old and is consistently the most prosperous department store chain of our nation, a fact not generally known because of the unique and totally private structure of the company. In a century the stores have had just two leaders: Mr. Belk and his second-eldest son, John M. Belk.

Mr. Belk came out of modest beginnings in Union County, North Carolina, with a large Presbyterian faith incorporating the Puritan work ethic and Calvinistic optimism, but he had few dollars. To accelerate growth, William Henry Belk handpicked managers that he made partners. In most instances they brought no money to the table, but they shared his vision, ambition, and integrity. Their stores were to offer better values and be the retail anchor of each city or town where they were located. The managers were to work hard, take an interest in civic and political affairs, and be recognized as regular attenders at the churches of their choice. Folklore has it that an entry interview with Mr. Belk included such a personal question as: "Are you a Christian . . . and a Presbyterian?" which most felt he considered synonymous! When Arthur Tyler responded, "I'm an Episcopalian," Mr. Belk mustered up all of his ecumenical grace and observed, "I knew *one* good one once, Arthur. You better be like him."

The driving force was that Mr. Belk made these early managers partners. He gave them the ownership of at least one-third of the store while he kept each store a separate corporation with a central buying service.

One of the last original partners is one of the greatest influences in my life, so beloved by our family that Edwin Colin Lindsey is simply "Uncle Colin." Born in Pelzer, South Carolina, over eight decades ago and raised in Mackintosh, Florida, so far "behind" the post office that when he flew to London on the *Concorde,* it took him the same amount of time as it once took him as a lad to hitch his mule to the wagon and go to town to fetch the mail. It is his Lindsey name that is hyphenated with Belk in Florida and Puerto Rico at thirty-five sites with the best volume and net return of various groups.

Mr. Belk early recognized Uncle Colin's ability to read people from an experience they shared outside of retailing. I witnessed this ability at a Board of Governors meeting of our THA Foundation (a foundation with the singular purpose of giving lucrative scholarships nationwide to financially needy young people who, upon graduation, will serve professionally in youth organizations such as scouting, YMCA, Boy's Clubs, and Girl's Clubs. Colin Lindsey and John Belk were part of the original twelve designers of the foundation).

Before this board of governors came a young man from Boston who showed great promise except for his obvious obesity which created a poor impression. While others held back, Uncle Colin quickly spoke up, "Poor chap, raised so poor on a steady starch diet that's all gone to his stomach. He sure needs our encouragement, and at college they'll give him a balanced diet." Unc was right. The young man trimmed down to become more attractive to interview committees and has written quite a chapter with Big Brothers/Big Sisters.

Such judgment isn't new for "Unc." At the close of World War II, in Winter Haven, where he opened his record-making store, "Unc" hired Del Funari, using the GI Bill offering split-dollars employment. "Every time I turned around, I bumped into Del," said Uncle Colin, "he was always at my shoulder learning everything I knew and much more. I figured he had just what I needed because he had ambition and 'guts.' " Here Del Funari was, a "minority"; an Italian in a small Anglo-Saxon town; a Catholic in an 85 percent Protestant county; a fast-talking Yankee in the heart of Florida's "cracker country." Today, upon Uncle Colin's retirement, Del heads the Belk-Lindsey group.

There is a great contrast between worldwide Coca-Cola and Florida's Belk-Lindsey stores, but there is also a great commonality of attitude. Mr. Lindsey's managers possess an almost religious loyalty toward him, although I have never heard him use the word or consider it a part of his measuring system. He not only paid them sound salaries but also large bonuses. His appraisal system wasn't annual, semi-annual, quarterly, or monthly. It was constant updates.

Here's the "grabber." As E. C. Lindsey gave them their sizable bonuses, often equaling or exceeding their salaries, he *never, never* allowed them to thank him. He told me, "If they thanked me, they'd have felt obligated to me. Instead, it was satisfying for me to say, 'I'm not giving you a gift. I'm proud to present you with what you've earned this year based on your fulfilling your commitment and much, much more. Thank you.' "

It was Unc's conviction that if he let them feel obligated, they might despise him. He wanted them to know he was only giving them *their* money which he felt didn't cost him a thing. What pragmatic praise! What a way for "Takin' Up The Slack."

How wise is this approach! Unable to thank Mr. Lindsey, the managers were motivated to do a better job the next year. If they didn't receive bonuses, the managers literally resigned themselves. Without bonuses they knew, without a word from Unc, that they lacked competence or had self-doubts or didn't like what they were doing or were bored or stagnant. The bonus told them and Uncle Colin how excited they were, what good planners they were, how strong they were in climbing over obstacles, how much inner drive they possessed, and how much proper pride they had.

What leverage Uncle Colin had! He threw all of his weight behind helping them look good. From their humble beginnings they were grateful to Mr. Belk for giving them a chance to gain identity and wealth. Unc's integrity demanded he pass the opportunity on. He built them up, raised his voice seldom, ranted never, but used the bonus as a pitch pipe to help his managers find the right note. Never have I witnessed such a dissimilar group of managers harmonizing on the same song.

Whether Coca-Cola or Belk, Don Keough or E. C. Lindsey, the underlining motive is the same. Goodness and fairness are not "carrot stick" mentality appealing to survival instincts. They are not "feathering their own nests" at the exclusion of their associates. It is a case of sharing the spirit. Literally blood, sweat, and tears are expended by those caught up in the drive, dynamism, and dedication of the leader's dream. They are immune to corporate narcissism that allows chewing up people to promote the leader's image.

They are moving among the wagon in the train, balancing the tangible and the intangible to fulfill different dreams with common endings.

9

No Travel This Day

"Sunday 13 July . . . Remained in camp today as we do not travel on Sundays. Gave rest to man and beast. After Bible, Ma mend up and wash clothes. Pa out for moss to fix the oxen hoof. Jedediah off hunting partridge. Prepare generally for the next weeks travel. Thunder showers in afternoon."

In diary after diary the Sunday entries of the pioneers are pretty much the same. A time for rest and rehabilitation for man and beast, it was also a time for prayer, for they had to reknit the unraveling of soul as well as body from the punishment of the trail.

In many of the formal rules governing the wagon trains, Sunday was singled out as a day of rest. Occasionally, the rule was broken when wagon trains had to cross a river or seek shelter of a nearby fort or get food. But the diary entry for the following Monday would show the price in frayed tempers, broken equipment, or disabled oxen that had to be paid.

The westering rule was to maintain the highest possible rate of travel commensurate with maintaining the strength of the draft animals and human health. To exceed that pace was to assure the ruin of the wagon train.

In fact conservation of energy was as important as its judicious expenditure. Even on a daily basis, rest was important. The midday "noonin'" break was not just a quick meal and then a racing forward. No, it was a four-hour event from 10:00 to 2:00 P.M. The high plains were possessed of a thin oxygen level, alkaline water, and dehydration that took its toll on everything and everyone. Pacing was important.

Rhythm: The Secret to a Winning Pace

Maybe we're determined not to learn from the past. During World War II our family was living near the Bethlehem shipyards of Quincy, Massachusetts. As the pace of the war quickened, the shipyards started working seven days a week, twenty-four hours a day, but productivity declined. Pausing and pacing are necessary for satisfactory performance. As children we heard, "Haste makes waste," and we thought it referred to doing numbers so quickly that we made careless arithmetic mistakes. Little did we understand that later in life it would mean trying to get everything done in such a frenzy that our efforts became fractional, pushing our bodies beyond the point of no return so any higher production numbers were negated by the poor quality of the work.

The Gospel of Matthew (11:28–30) contains one of the warmest invitations of Jesus: "Come to Me, all you who labor and are heavy laden, and I will give you rest. Take My yoke upon you and learn from Me, for I am gentle and lowly in heart, and you will find rest for your souls. For My yoke is easy and My burden is light."

Contrary to common application, Jesus is not inviting His disciples to join Him in inactivity and escape but to develop restful work habits. He wants them to change from the "gray fatigue," where one goes to bed tired and gets up feeling worse, to "glowing fatigue" where one is tired yet satisfied, where sleep is peaceful and refreshing. Jesus is not saying that we ought to escape the yoke of responsibility or the burden of labor; He is saying that if our lives are in rhythm, the yoke becomes a flattering collar and the burden, a blessing. Whether we wake to a sunrise, listen to the tide, watch the changing of the seasons, or hear the chirping of a bird amidst the storm, our universe shares God's rhythm, and our faith to follow His example, increases our effectiveness to the extent that we imitate the divine pace of the Creator of it all.

The writers of books and lectures on time management

have been prolific. Unfortunately, the majority of them deal more with style than with substance. The majority emphasize recordkeeping to assure forcibly the use of every minute and prevent the waste of time. Thus theoretically they can get more done than anyone else. Unfortunately, each idle moment tends to give them a sense of guilt. If they are not careful, they become servants to the system rather than wiser time stewards. The system, once in place, causes a tension resulting from the tendency to self-condemn themselves for any break in their stride. This leads to self-imposed robotic action identified more with action than with achievement.

Life proceeds in rhythm. Without it, we lose flexibility and creativity.

We can possess all the good executive characteristics of determination, tough-mindedness, hard work, intelligence, analytical ability—but it all goes for naught without rhythm.

Without a harmonious life, we limit our choices; become afraid of variations; fail to develop fresh approaches or new options. We like to brag about the workaholic who can swim against the tide, but I have never observed a person going against the tide when the tide didn't win.

The late President John F. Kennedy, who was fond of quoting from the wisdom of King Solomon, found these words in Ecclesiastes 3:1–8:

<blockquote>
To everything there is a season,
A time for every purpose under heaven:
A time to be born,
And a time to die;
A time to plant,
And a time to pluck what is planted;
A time to kill,
And a time to heal;
A time to break down,
And a time to build up;
A time to weep,
And a time to laugh;
</blockquote>

A time to mourn,
And a time to dance;
A time to cast away stones,
And a time to gather stones;
A time to embrace,
And a time to refrain from embracing;
A time to gain,
And a time to lose;
A time to keep,
And a time to throw away;
A time to tear,
And a time to sew;
A time to keep silence,
And a time to speak;
A time to love,
And a time to hate;
A time of war,
And a time of peace.

Uncle Howard's "Hook-ups"

To my Uncle Howard Irvin, I owe a great debt. Actually, it is more like many debts as he and Aunt Kathleen became my surrogate parents during a period of my student life in Greenville, South Carolina.

Along with my scholarship, I needed some spending money. The Irvins were in the used car sales business. Uncle Howard purchased most of his stock from new car dealers in the Greater Pittsburgh area. During World War II, cars were kept in better condition there. The only cars that sold profitably in Greenville were Fords and Chevrolets. He would drive a Buick Roadmaster or a Chrysler New Yorker to Pittsburgh, trade even for the same year Ford or Chevy, and make a profit at the Greenville auction.

So Uncle Howard invited me during the off season to fly to Pittsburgh and drive a "hook-up" back to Greenville. Not only did it give me spending money, but it also introduced me to commercial flying and established in my mind that mine would be an age where I could live where I wanted and fly to where I needed to work. (That perception came back to me a few years ago when Colonel Frank Borman asked me to be an advisor to Eastern.) In 1949 I would go to Pittsburgh after classes at noon on Friday, flying on a DC-3 that had departed Atlanta and had already stopped at Anderson before I boarded in Greenville. It would stop at Spartanburg 20 miles away; 60 more miles at Charlotte; 65 more miles to Winston-Salem; 20 miles to Greensboro/High Point; then a long 110 miles to Roanoke; 100 more miles to Huntington; and finally our straight shot to Pittsburgh! That was the direct flight! I thought it was great. We never flew over the mountains; we flew around them. At Charlotte, they gave us a box lunch. By Roanoke, we gave it back! If we weren't bouncing, we knew we weren't flying. Of course, the DC-3 was the safest plane ever manufactured. It never killed; it just occasionally made us wish we were dead!

The fun came driving the cars back home. Have you ever driven a hook-up of two cars made in 1940, cars that had been driven through the war years, cars that weren't owned by "little ole schoolmarms"? First, the motors were suspect; the brakes were "happenchance"; and there was "play" in the steering. I would leave Pittsburgh, take the Pennsylvania Turnpike to Breezewood; cut through a corner of West Virginia to Winchester, Virginia; down the Shenandoah Valley to Roanoke, past my present home in High Point, and on to Greenville, arriving in time for a Saturday noon class.

What made the cars salable by Uncle Howard were clean upholstery, unmarred seats, and unrusted window sticks. The motors could be replaced with a $65 special from Sears. The steering could be tightened—in Greenville! Out I started, though, from Pittsburgh with a shimmy in the steering and a jury-rigged braking system. My enemy was the uneven swaying of the two cars and the challenge of negotiating the mountain curves. Going around those curves, many without guardrails, I would feel the cars creep toward the gravel shoulders. I knew if I tensed and yanked the steering wheel, I would flip over. Gently, I would prod the hook-up back toward the white line, but not over it lest I hit oncoming traffic. I found myself talking to myself: "Relax, sense the rhythm of the hooked, swaying cars. If I don't get into the rhythm of the flow, I won't make it."

You can't imagine how many times, when I have confronted crisis, been blindsided by the unexpected, faced an apparent dead end, I have stopped and pictured myself driving one of Uncle Howard's hook-ups, listening for the rhythm of the situation.

"Mr. Yellow Pages"—Loren Berry

In more recent years I had another tutor, the late Loren M. Berry, "Mr. Yellow Pages," who died "young" in his ninety-second year. He isn't an example of "pacing" simply because he lived a long life. Confucius said that some people die old at thirty while others are youthful at ninety. Given the privilege to be the master of ceremonies at his ninetieth birthday, I was sitting by a man who never considered retirement or death and was daily at his desk planning for the days ahead.

Here was a man left fatherless at the age of 4 when his father, a school principal, died of typhoid fever. His mother, who lived to be 104, was left to raise him, maintaining the home by working as a seamstress, a door-to-door distributor of medicine supplies, and a $5-a-day maternity nurse. Loren Berry began his selling at age 8 delivering horseradish he dug from a creek. He cleaned, ground, bottled, and sold it for 5¢ a jar. At the same time, he began delivering newspapers, selling subscriptions to *The Saturday Evening Post;* and he also had a laundry route.

While in high school, Berry worked on his hometown newspaper, *The Wabash Plain Dealer*, as a $3-a-week reporter. He also served as the sports editor and business manager for his school monthly. While still in high school he started selling timetables for interurban railroads, soliciting advertising to pay for the printing. Soon he was traveling the major cities of the midwest pushing the sale of his vest-pocket timetable idea. One of his timetable clients in Marion, Indiana, owned the local telephone service and asked Loren Berry if he couldn't help him prepare his telephone number listings in a way that would make advertising more profitable. The "Yellow Pages" were born.

In the next seventy years this little man of about five feet became a giant of enterprise and joined that illustrious group of Dayton, Ohioans, that included his friends, Charles Kettering, John Patterson, and Tom Watson. Looking into his warm, soft eyes, you saw a man with a heart bigger than his body and the spirit of a champion.

When I was chronicling his life on film in 1977, I asked him to explain, among other things, why his company leaped forward during the Depression years and why, long after most men retire, he had, with his able son John, opened up their international business with his pal, Harold Geneen.

As to the Depression, he replied, "Tom, I had something my clients needed, really needed at that time: the best value in advertising. I was so busy delivering what they needed that I just let the newspapers and the economic professors worry about the Depression. To my memory, I never used the word or considered we were having one. I was too busy."

And as to why he was still working, Loren replied with a twinkle in his eye, "You know my son John is now chairman and I'm vice chairman. With this inflation we're having, it costs a lot to live and John holds pretty tight salary reins, so I must keep working!" After a soft chuckle, he became totally serious and said quickly and humbly, "I've been fortunate to know many people who have shared with me a faith in the individual's ability to achieve; a willingness to work hard, very hard; and a strong belief in the free enterprise system. I've still got much to do to justify their confidence and my way is to keep looking forward and upward for new opportunities for the fine people scattered throughout our country and around the world who carry the banner of the L. M. Berry Company. Surely, you of all people, Tom, don't think God put us here to just arbitrarily quit, do you?"

The interview stopped for a moment for a tape change for the TV camera. We were in the backyard of Mr. Berry's modest and extremely comfortable home, sitting under a big tree— the same spreading tree that the Wright Brothers played around as kids. Quite suddenly he closed his eyes and was off on a four-minute nap. Just as quickly he was totally alert again as the camera started rolling.

Mr. Berry helped me form some ideas about pacing regardless of our age.

1. *From the age of eight when he started selling, he kept a daily diary complete with meticulous financial records.* Writing each evening meant he closed his business daily. He measured life "full-day by full-day" but never considered he was getting behind, for each day became history as soon as it was recorded. Each morning consequently became a fresh, clean, unwritten sheet of life. As much as any person I have met, he never allowed himself the luxury of unfinished business or the frustration of playing "catch-up ball." This meant he napped often and slept soundly. He told me he couldn't remember but very few nights when he wasn't asleep within five minutes after his head hit the pillow.

2. *Honesty was never an option but an obligation.* He never cluttered his mind worrying about what he said nor concerned himself with embellishing his own image.

3. *Asked by one reporter when he realized he had made it in the business world, he replied, "I never thought about it.* We were growing so fast and there's so much opportunity, I just never thought about it."

"Is it true," the reporter inquired, "that you're worth a half billion dollars?"

Laughingly, Mr. Berry said, "John now controls the purse. If you're right, I need a raise." It was not false humility, but Mr. Berry's mission didn't start, nor was it motivated by, nor did it end with the size of his bank account. He had a mission.

4. *He kept life simple because he had a profound mind.* Those who can see clearly are able to remove the clutter of confusion and fuzziness from their life. As Rebecca West observes, the trouble many of us have is that "man is twofold. He cannot learn truths which are too complicated; he forgets truths which are too simple."

Reread what Mr. Berry said about the Depression. As in all great companies, his growth was finest when times were toughest. The respected Bill Fetridge, Chairman of Dartnell, confirmed to me that *Depression* was not a dinner subject during the 1930s. There was too much to do.

Mr. Berry's removal of clutter led to a total restructuring of my own morning hours. Now I don't read a newspaper until noon or watch a morning TV news/talk show. When have you read the morning paper and felt better? The late Chief Justice

Earl Warren, didn't go quite as far as I, but he said, "I always turn first to the sports pages, which record people's accomplishments. The front page has nothing but man's failures."

Bill Gove, one of the platform speaker's real refreshments, told me: "I've instructed Gloria that if she sees the start of World War III on *Good Morning, America,* first tell me how the Red Sox did before such gossip." I am convinced that starting a day hearing news of events I could not change, watching tragedies that were impossible to correct, filling my stomach with caffeine, all meant I went to the office with a spirit dragging and energy impaired. A free society depends on upbeat moods.

Many respected thinkers understand this need and are concerned about seeing a healthy society buffeted by what Lionel Trilling called an "adversary culture," where we are exposed to so much gloom about our modern democratic life that our confidence is undermined and we are robbed of our vigor. The coalition of print and TV can steal the magic of hope from us.

Loren Berry wasn't blind to reality, but he wouldn't tolerate propaganda clothed as news. He rejected the negative media hysteria in his later years and felt we could go to the moon before we did. He believed we could cure cancer, erase illiteracy, improve the quality of life for all, and sell our system over Russia's to the world. Whenever I had the least touch of hysteria over a reported development, I would call him to find he was planning his next step forward.

5. *People never turned his head.* Outside of God, the greatest person he knew was his mother; all others paled by comparison. That is why he could be so much help to people like Senator Robert Taft, our presidents, and fellow titans of business. He saw people as people. Eating at Joe's Crabs in Miami was as exciting to him as being at 1600 Pennsylvania Avenue. "Mr. Republican" with democratic eyes, he never wasted time trying to impress anyone except a customer he wanted to help. He knew Rudyard Kipling's lines:

> If you can talk with crowds and keep your virtue,
> Or walk with Kings—nor lose the common touch,

153

If neither foes nor loving friends can hurt you,
If all men count with you, but none too much . . . .

6. *Loren hurried but was never harried.* He kept a methodical schedule but never made others feel rushed. At close of day, he could relax totally playing a piano, which he learned to do as a background musician for the silent movies, or laughing at us for not being able to catch his magic tricks. At his customer parties one never had the feeling of being a guest but rather the warmth of being a family member.

7. *He lived deeply and knew love was eternal while life was temporal.* He gave generously to worthy causes, especially those related to young people, for he realized that here was the only way anyone crosses century lines. Today, in our THA Foundation, as in a multitude of other places, young people are in college because of a Loren M. Berry endowment. His son John shares the partnership they enjoyed in heart as well as business, for in the same spirit he has given multimillion-dollar gifts to places like his alma mater.

What all this adds up to is that I met in Loren M. Berry a man who never heard the word *bored.* Somehow we think pioneers like him have such a varied life that of course they were not bored. Wrong! When we heap one achievement upon another, they have the sameness of "routine labor." Mr. Berry, near the end of his earthly sojourn, told me he couldn't understand "executive burn-out." He personifies to me these encouraging words from the prophet Isaiah

> But those who wait on the LORD
> Shall renew their strength;
> They shall mount up with wings like eagles,
> They shall run and not be weary,
> They shall walk and not faint.
>
> (Isaiah 40:31)

As I write I see the honor I had sitting by Loren M. Berry at Super Foods' corporate board meetings. He had done it all! What others considered impossible, he made routine; and because he understood the rhythm of life, he wore a mischievous grin with the freshness of a Hoosier kid who built assets on the boulders others would call liabilities.

How can we achieve such a pleasing rhythm in life? Let's examine several key factors.

I. The Reality Factor

Life is difficult. This is a great truth, one of the greatest truths. It is a great truth because once we truly see this truth, *we transcend it*. Once we truly know that life is difficult; once we truly understand and accept it, then life is no longer difficult. Because once it is accepted, *the fact that life is difficult no longer matters (emphasis added)*.

Dr. M. Scott Peck, *The Road Less Traveled*,
(New York: Simon and Schuster, 1978).

Jesus said, "In the world you will have tribulation; but be of good cheer, I have overcome the world."

The first of Buddha's *Four Noble Truths* was: "Life is suffering."

President Jimmy Carter was considered profound for saying, "Life isn't fair."

On Christmas 1985 ABC's *Nightline* opined that the "Baby Boomers" are having a rough time because they're expecting too much. We led them to this. We forgot that we enjoyed the journey. So the Yuppies naturally feel they should have a "fail-safe" society.

The journey of life is an excitement as long as we keep our destination in mind. Have you visited the Bok Singing Tower in Central Florida? If so, you might remember that one of the benches on which you can sit and meditate has this quotation from P. E. Burroughs: "I come here to find myself. It is so easy to get lost in the world."

In an earlier chapter, I wrote of the wagon train's map. We cannot be declared lost unless we first have a goal and a plan to reach it. Still having all this in place doesn't insure us from wandering off course on our journey. Bunyan's *Pilgrim's Progress* has a message for any traveler: the exhilaration of achievement is in direct proportion to the number of pitfalls we have missed at best or climbed out of at worst.

Distress has become the mental common cold of our era.

Distress is probably found in one per one thousand of our population. Unfortunately, although rare, the cold that starts with fever, chest pain, cough, and congestion leads to pneumonia. Our effort is to stop distress before it leads to extreme depression. You will note, I use the word *distress*, not *stress*.

Included in my reading each week are a dozen periodicals, not including newspapers and "inside" newsletters. In addition, I interrupt my book reading on planes to at least skim each magazine available. I cannot name one magazine that hasn't had at least one article related to stress during the last twelve months, including even the traditional home magazines featuring garden and home furnishings. Knowing that more and more people feel their jobs are impossible and their families uncontrollable, the outside world keeps testing to see if we have become a shockproof society.

So we have turned inside to ourselves. We call it self-improvement, but it is really self-escape. What we call a "new birth of conservatism" among young executives may simply be the birth of "looking out for number 1." The pious overtone is, "If I don't value myself, then how can I be of value to another?" The truth is, in trying to find an acceptable self, people may be forgetting others. To paraphrase Thackeray, "The world is a looking-glass, and gives back to every man the reflection of his own thought."

In attempting to declare distress invalid, instead of working through it, the translation is:

> Permissive society is in; guilt, sin, and punishment are
>   out.
> Indulgence is in; authority is out.
> Leisure is in; long hours are out.
> Spending is in; saving is out.
> Role-playing is in; service and responsibility are out.
> Therapy is in; worship is out.
> Superficiality is in; sincerity is out.
> Understanding is in; commitment is out.

As *Fortune* magazine suggested, we're becoming "a cautious, subdued generation that will not stick its neck out. It keeps its shirt on . . . its chin up . . . and its mouth shut."

So we have distress and we have come to Carl Jung's diagnosis: "Neurosis is always a substitute for legitimate suffering." This neurotic distress causes us to replace aggressiveness with surliness. Once creative, our minds become sluggish. Cynicism replaces humor. Complacency replaces inquisitiveness. Fuzziness replaces concentration. Surrender replaces risk. Passivity replaces impatience. We dread opening mail or answering the phone lest we are asked to do something more or are reminded of what we failed to do. Eating alone becomes desirable. Withdrawal replaces activism.

What are the warning signals about distress?

1. *Your ego makes you think everything should run smoothly.* Who are you to think you can escape problems—or should? The late B. C. Forbes revealed his stringent Scottish raising in the following: "Difficulties, like work, are blessings in disguise. Life would become monotonous, colorless, deadening without them. Difficulties should act as a tonic, spur us to greater exertion, strengthen our willpower. Study the subject through to the bottom, and you will arrive at the conclusion: 'Thank God for difficulties.' "

Maeterlinck once advised: "The beginning of wisdom is the acknowledgment of our creaturehood." Distress is the ultimate folly of those who deny their creaturehood. Creaturehood suggests insecurity, inadequacy, mortality, finiteness, limitations. It means we are limited by time, space, physical weakness, disease, lack of knowledge. Human life is basically fragile and insecure.

No matter how often you read your own press release, accept the reality that there are days that start out bad and then the bottom falls out!

2. *Distress comes when you have a sense of inadequacy.* It can be that you are better than you admit or accept, but you have adopted standards beyond your abilities. You have a perfectionist nature. You know the perfectionist—he takes pains and gives them to others! It could be you are overly ambitious. You have connived and politicked for your job. Now you have it, and you're scared! Our problems seldom stem from what we want to be but often from what we fear we aren't.

3. *Distress comes when you think you can go it alone.* We are interrelated. We all are Siamese. Although you may feel part

157

of your distress is caused by others, delegating to others may be a solution. Never, never were you and I designed to be gods but always, always we need God and His wisdom. We are not messiahs but people. A bleeding ulcer isn't the badge of battle success.

Effectiveness isn't measured by what we accomplish as much as by what we relinquish.

Ants are achievers because they organize and work together. Dr. Mike Debakey surrounds himself with the best medical team. Policemen patrol in pairs at night. Foxholes are dug for two.

How J. C. Penney Won over Worry

As the Crash of '29 was echoing, J. C. Penney felt somewhat smug about his business. He thought he was depression-proof with the majority of his stores in small towns away from the fray. He had unfortunately made some unwise personal commitments that overtaxed his strength. He felt he had to carry the business on his own broad shoulders. Conscientious, he became too worried to sleep. He came down with painful shingles. Though hospitalized and given sedatives, he still experienced only limited relief as he tossed all night. The combination of circumstances had broken him so completely, physically and mentally, that he now viewed death as a real possibility and wrote farewell letters to his wife and son.

To his surprise and joy, he made it through that dark Saturday night and was awakened from a welcomed, sound sleep by the singing in the hospital chapel:

> Be not dismayed whate'er betide,
> God will take care of you;
> Beneath His wings of love abide,
> God will take care of you;
> Through days of toil when heart doth fail,
> God will take care of you;

When dangers fierce your path assail,
God will take care of you;
No matter what may be the test,
God will take care of you;
Lean, weary one, upon His breast,
God will take care of you.

In Rock Hill in 1952, I heard Mr. Penney recall this incident at the occasion of a luncheon signaling his renovated store opening. He said: "The hymn was followed by Scripture reading and prayer. Suddenly, something happened. I can't explain it. I can only call it a miracle. I felt as if I had been instantly lifted out of the darkness of a dungeon into warm, brilliant, sunlight. I felt as if I had been transported from hell to paradise. I felt the power of God as I never felt it before. I realized then that I alone was responsible for my troubles. I knew that God with His love was there to help me. He would minister to me through the people working with me in our stores."

"From that day to this," Mr. Penney continued, "my life has been free from worry. I am now seventy-seven years old, and the most dramatic and glorious minutes of my life were those spent in that hospital overhearing the chapel service that morning."

I'm not suggesting we use God as an escape or a cop-out; but I do recommend we accept that life is a rhythm which can produce sour music if we try to go it alone, or get out of sync with our Creator. A novelist once wrote: "I'm not an 8-day clock. I run down in 24 hours and have to be rewound."

Leaders are under the constant pressure for action. As James F. Bere of Borg-Warner said to the Harvard Business School Club: "If you can't take time to lean back and think and plan, you are neither leading or managing; you are simply being driven."

II. The Resolution Force

I still have difficulty accepting that some people enjoy keeping their lives out of rhythm. If they don't have a crisis, they will create one. They want life off balance. If my ancient Aunt Fadwah couldn't think of something to worry about, she worried herself crazy until she did. Do you know people like that?

We grew up visiting Uncle Wayne and Aunt Edith. They weren't really relatives but classmates of my parents who became family to us. They were blessed with eight children.

One day Aunt Edith looked out from the upstairs of their large home in Darlington, Maryland, and saw half a dozen other children lying on their stomachs in a circle around something. With a mother's curiosity, she went to another window where she could almost overlook them. She gasped as she realized they were studying baby skunks! Opening the window she screamed, "Children, run!" They did. Each picked up a baby skunk by the tail and took off!

If you enjoy misery, then life is potentially stinking, isn't it? Charles Haddon Spurgeon wrote a century ago: "Anxiety does not empty tomorrow of its sorrows, but only empties today of its strength."

How can we avoid crippling anxiety?

1. *Learn from yesterday; look forward to tomorrow.* If we accept Scott Peck's statement that "life is difficult," then we should resolve that, after we go through each difficulty, we learn from it, but still face forward. This is what the late Dr. E. Stanley Jones observed about the first-century church: "They didn't say, 'Look what the world is coming to.' They didn't empha-size the question. They presented the answer, 'Look what has come to the world.' " They were an example for us that we can not only find rhythm in our lives but also "help the whole world to sing" as well.

2. *Take life seriously but not ourselves.* What we need is not a tensionless state but a striving for a goal bigger than our-selves. What Dean Wickes commented about to students at Princeton years ago applies to us as well. He wasn't excited when a student *understood* a great idea as much as when a student was *captured* by a profound idea.

I'm probably the only speaker on the circuit who encour-ages people to get *more* stress to prevent distress. We know that medicines, except for placebos, are usually regulated poisons to ward off greater poisons. So stress, or getting caught up in work, prevents distress. Stress is being conscientious in work, almost losing oneself in it. Distress comes by keeping the world in orbit around oneself so each event is followed by, "Why me?" or "Why not me?" Self-centeredness and paranoia are part of distress; stress is outgoing.

CBS and Tom Wyman

In 1980 came the announcement that Thomas H. Wyman had been recruited to the presidency of CBS. When I called to congratulate him I also said, "Tom, if I were a betting man and could find a bookie, I'd lay odds that you'll soon go on to being chairman and CEO with Mr. Paley's endorsement and enthusiasm." So what? Predictable? Not so! From the moment Dr. Frank Stanton learned he would be forced to retire from being president and COO after years of sharing the building of CBS, there had been a succession of pretenders to the throne, only to be denied and dismissed. To Tom would go the mantle.

You might say that it's just another case where preparation and opportunity met. Indeed they did. Like a successful mountain climber, Tom learned early in life that stocking the base camp is as important as having the stamina to make the climb.

From his modest raising in St. Louis, Tom Wyman became a Phi Beta Kappa student at Amherst, graduating magna cum laude as an English major. More important than his choice of a major was his college resolution that he would assign himself to missions in life worthy of draining his physical, mental, and emotional energies. Satisfaction would come in his exertions. He started his career climb in the international section of what then was New York's First National Bank. Gaining a worldwide perspective, he moved up to become the fair-haired boy of the world-class Nestlé Company. We then watched him become the trainer who built the muscles of the Jolly Green Giant and at the appropriate time moved the Jolly Green Giant to its domicile at the Pillsbury Company.

Tom was raised listening to America's best-managed radio station, KMOX, the CBS flagship in St. Louis, never dreaming he would one day receive the mantle of William Paley. By 1980

Mr. Paley was rightfully a legend in his own time, for he had shaped the radio and television industry to his own image. As a media observer said, "The other two networks won't be satisfied equaling CBS in the ratings; they want to be CBS." He had built his network dynasty upside down, simplifying the contracts with the affiliates. He didn't see them just as enhancing CBS's bottom line but also as lead programmers. With their support, he was not reluctant to give them Hall of Fame talent like Jack Benny, Bing Crosby, Red Skelton, George Burns and Gracie Allen, Will Rogers, Edgar Bergen, and Kate Smith. Often he let them prove themselves on another network before wooing them away. Even at equal salary, CBS meant a promotion. Bill Paley had that sixth sense. Loving the arts, he could applaud Beverly Sills at the opera one night and the next day sign *The Beverly Hillbillies*. He could encourage Van Cliburn's genius one minute and stomp his foot with "Fats" Waller the next.

The newsroom became the living room at CBS. If Bill Paley was the soul of CBS, then Edward R. Murrow was the heart. *60 Minutes* would be a mainstay at the top of the ratings. Walter Cronkite, with his gravelly voice could put on the robes of CBS and become the most trusted man in television.

When C. P. Snow mourned that the arrival of Sputnik stripped the bachelor of arts degree of life and made the bachelor of science an oracle, it was Bill Paley who helped us understand how we can use the fundamentals of science to preserve the arts.

Tom Wyman came into the arena of William Paley, the man who could balance the sublime with the ridiculous, who could have us stroking our brow over *Omnibus* or belly laughing at Jackie Gleason; who could provide step-by-step coverage of Selma or laughter at baldheaded Archie Bunker.

Why was Tom desperately needed? Like the select few who literally birth an industry, Bill Paley used to excess the entrepreneur privilege of being too busy to be bothered with the mundane—like profit and loss or bottom lines. After all, TV was riding high. Mistakes were buried under too many piles of dollars to be found and used as beneficial learning experiences for the future. With an ego that wouldn't accommodate second best, CBS News had convinced a collection of attractive, good readers with a writer for every two words that they were astute newsmen. He had created a giant too big for life.

Bill Paley wasn't unaware of the potential dangers. As a master of timing, he knew when to ride out a storm, when he could do no wrong, and when to leave it to a successor to see if he could do any right. So to Tom Wyman, with his natural modesty and native instincts that made him always under-promise and overproduce, fell the task of preserving William Paley's honor while trimming CBS to fighting weight, effectively facing the competition of the changing media battle.

The climate Tom Wyman faced was just as new and pioneering as Bill Paley's first radio station. The choice of Tom was good because he had never taken himself seriously. He was as comfortable attending a PTA meeting for his children as being rushed through New York in a stretch limo. He saw his mission not as image building but corporation maturing. He would let Bill Paley be the shining knight on the white horse while he cleaned the stable. Never have I called Tom when he sounded harassed or impatient. Just before leaving CBS, he was still making the moves he felt were necessary.

It was Tom Wyman who had the audacity to feel that newspeople should do their own research and pound their own typewriters. Authenticity, he believed, would smooth out the rough spots. Now he had struck a nerve. We who listen to news realize the personalities doing the reporting are too cloistered to understand business and too pampered to appreciate practicality. In his wildest imagination no one would see Andy Rooney as an executive, but he became one of the honest "trigger men" who cried out that the CBS News couldn't keep its high ratings if he and his colleagues were expected to do their own writing. The network felt no sense of the changing broadcast economy nor any blame for the frontal attacks of Senator Jesse Helms or maverick Ted Turner.

They played into the hands of another group, coming as wolves in sheep's clothing that hid their real agenda. Borrowing a title from ABC, they revived the "Fall Guy," only as Tom Wyman. Bill Paley was brought out for window dressing only to realize in less than ninety days that he had been duped. The cuts Tom knew to be necessary for a long-term strategy were now done with a dull, blunt instrument.

Tom Wyman was disappointed but not bitter after the change. In the heat of the struggle, Tom showed his balanced outlook by accepting the chairmanship of the trustees of his alma mater as well as joining the board of an international conglomerate. As he sits sorting out the wave of offers, Tom just proves the force and balance of someone who feels life is both a gift and disappointment. He has never given the impression of being unhappy in his work. Actually, I never found him wasting time asking, "Am I happy or unhappy?" Instead, his time is spent thinking about what has to be done and what it takes to do it. Now this is the resolution force of a paced life. As a Bible teacher taught me, "You work your work; don't let your work work you."

III. The Recreation Formula

Today's "health kick" is here to stay. The fallacy is that we are becoming one-dimensional monstrosities. The question is not how long we can preserve the body but if we can renew the mind to keep ourselves recreating. The forces that curb leadership are more internal than external. J.B. Phillips translates St. Paul's instruction to the Romans: "Don't let the world around you squeeze you into its own mold, but let God remold your minds from within, so that you may prove in practice that the plan of God for you is good, meets all his demands and moves toward the goal of true maturity [leadership]" (12:2).

Recreating our lives daily depends on:

1. *A life recreated with simple philosophy.* One of the most fascinating leadership philosophies I have ever encountered was that of Joe Gilbert, founder of Gilbert/Robinson restaurants headquartered in Kansas City, Missouri. You may have eaten in one of his fifty Houlihan's Old Place, or Annie's Santa Fe or perhaps Captain Jeremiah Tuttle, the Bristol Bar and Grille, or the famed Plaza III. Joe's restaurants were never alike, each having its own distinctiveness, its own decor package, and its own leadership class operation. That's no easy task when you operate over eighty leading establishments.

Joe started weaving his pattern early on when he turned around a losing hot dog stand. He grew up on the ragged edge of life. He fretted not about yesterday, nor was he overwhelmed thinking about tomorrow. A day at a time was sufficient. Reminiscing at age eighty-two, he confided to me in his luxurious offices: "Tom, I enjoy these new offices. I look at these artifacts and each brings back pleasant memories. Each picture is worth a thousand words of history. But I have to confess that I am no more excited now, sitting here in this lovely new headquarters building, than I was each step of the way. But I am no less excited either.

"When I got my first job as a dishwasher, it was exciting. When I became a sweeper, it was exciting—a cook's helper, a baker's apprentice, a fry cook, and finally an owner —it was all exciting, challenging, and, yes, hazardous to me.

"The fear of losing this corporation with all its restaurants is no greater than the fear I had of losing my first job or my first management responsibility.

"I have a little monitor, you see. Whenever I find myself walking around with my hand shoved deep in my pocket, it's a clear signal pressures are getting to me. So I straighten my back and lift the level of my chin. There's no time to shuffle around feeling sorry for myself."

Joe's system worked. His restaurant group became so recognized that Peter Grace made him an offer he couldn't refuse and bought him out. Peter became so proud of the acquisition that on an occasion when European guests arrived at his New York home, he flew them in his corporate jet to Kansas City so they could have, of all things, 1,500 miles inland, "spectacular seafood" at the Bristol Bar and Grille.

Just before leaving for Switzerland, Joe told me he didn't feel at eighty-four that the Grace Company would renew his contract, nor should they, so, "Tom, I look to you for a meaningful opportunity with your lecturing work; I'm too young to quit." The last phone call he made was from Switzerland to my office. How Kansas City misses an integral artery of their civic heart! How I miss my "Pal Joey!" He would say that any achievement was credited to God, to Millie, his love and partner, and to a simple personal creed by which he recreated himself:

- Thank people who do good things, even if they're not doing them directly to you. And take time each day to write notes to those who deserve a pat on the back.
- Take time to talk to those you work with each day.
- If someone has a problem, really listen to them before you give an answer.
- It's not my business if you smoke, but I don't like what cigarettes may do to you.
- Fill your life so full of the positive that there's no room for the negative.
- Remember your company is only as good as your employees.
- When you make a mistake, don't dwell on it. Ask yourself instead: "What have I learned from it and what can I do now to grow from the mistake?"
- Don't ever stop seeking ways to grow and help others grow.
- Have confidence in those you work with, and express that confidence regularly.
- Don't verbalize your problems to the world. Be so full of concern for others that you don't have room for burdening them with yours.

While we have "institutionalized" leadership, the Joe Gilberts of this world remind us that life is still a personal affair. We tend to measure the position a person holds. Joe believed the person must position himself. We often feel that if a person is a leader in an excellent company, he must be excellent; but Judas refuted that 1900 years ago. In understanding the professional leader, we cannot afford to shift our admiration from the person to the position. It is the person who has sense, skill, and strength. It's the person who, as Frank Borman would say, "must earn his wings every day."

No matter what the size or shape of the corporation, it still takes on the style of the leader. Joe Gilbert we would classify an entrepreneur, and I would retain the same compliment for John H. Stafford at Pillsbury. He is everything but the caretaker we think professional executives are. Coming from a background with Kentucky Fried Chicken and the Green Giant Company, he assumed the helm of Pillsbury with a defined personal philosophy that he externalized in four succinct promises to the company's public:

1. We will ship to you what you order.
2. We will ship you the quality that we promised.
3. We will ship you when we said we'd deliver.
4. We will charge you what we agreed together.

There is an underlying foundation to the philosophies of Joe and Jack and all respected leaders: integrity. Integrity is the basis for self-esteem. Self-concept determines destiny: "Character determines action." When integrity is our keystone, our philosophy of living becomes wondrously simple. Severe simplicity and lack of adornment make for this attractive living. Book I of Plato's *Republic* confirms, "Beauty of style and harmony of grace and good rhythm depend on simplicity."

2. *A life is recreated with strategic pauses.* Tom Allsopp taught me the true meaning of the real world. He convinced me that it was necessary to have strategic pauses to increase one's effectiveness. Tom could well have been thinking in line with Rollo May: "It is an old and ironic habit of human beings to run faster when we have lost our way." Probably more correctly he wanted me to escape the fate observed by Henry Thoreau of Walden Pond: "The mass of men lead lives of quiet desperation."

I first met Tom through our mutual interest in the Boy Scouts of America. Tom was then heading the Northeast Home Office for Prudential Life. His offices at the Prudential/Sheraton Center had been raised from the ashes of urban squalor in downtown Boston. For the "Pru," the Northeast Home Office had at best been an "also ran." Tom had brought it to national leadership.

In a crucial December when most in his role would be whipping his "sales horses" into a frenzy to sell one more policy ("Help people give a Christmas gift to themselves. Be sure they take advantage of the year-end and defer as much of their income as possible."), Tom closed up shop and arranged for all of the employees to have an exclusive night with Arthur Fiedler and the Boston Pops, a strategic pause that would actually assure increased productivity.

After closing a record year, while most executives would be in a dither to beat their best, Tom responded to a request to be a guest lecturer at Tufts.

Tom was teaching me that the "real world" is neither frenzy

nor relaxation, acceleration nor coasting, Boston nor the Cape, running nor resting. The "real world" is balance, rhythm, pacing, circling the wagons. He was reminding me of a wall plaque in an old country store of the South:

Don't run too fast.
You'll run by more than you'll ever catch.

This is much like the statement of Fletcher Byron, Chairman of Koppers: "Our theory is that the best motivated person is a 5'10" nonswimmer in 6 feet of water. If you're doing as well as you should be, your head ought to be a little bit under the water all of the time. People perform best under conditions of moderate tension." I agree, but I am sure Fletcher would have been the first to say we must also come out of the water occasionally if we are to survive.

Grenville Kleiser sagely advised, "When your day is largely made up of energetic concentrated effort, provide for periods of complete relaxation when you can take it easy and recharge your batteries.

As my dad entered his ninetieth year, I recalled how ahead of his day he had been in maintaining his energy. When I was a lad, Dad had a favorite rocker which he possessed with the tenacity that Archie Bunker did his. Later he found a child-size rocker so I could sit beside him and rock. On occasion Dad would say, "Tommy, I'm going to do something for you now, and you'll thank me all of your life. I want you to sit and take a five-minute nap with me." You can imagine, of course, how distasteful this was to a bouncing, growing, energetic boy.

Dad would say, "Now sit comfortably, both feet on the floor, arms resting on the arm rests, and take three deep breaths with me." He was teaching me to breathe from my diaphragm, then he'd continue, "Say to your head, 'Relax and hang loosely.' Say to your shoulders, 'Relax and slump' (the only time he tolerated slumping). Tell your arms, 'relax'; legs, 'relax'; toes, 'relax'." Seldom did I hear the last instructions, for I was asleep. I am not certain he finished before he was asleep as well. Try it sometime.

How grateful I am now. I can be asleep before the plane

leaves the ground. For someone destined to average five hours of sleep nightly, napping has been the energy source for turning the adrenaline on full blast. Often awakening from the brief pauses, I recall words from the prophet Isaiah: "In returning and rest, you shall be saved;/ In quietness and confidence shall be your strength" (30:15).

This I couple with the hymn lines:

> Drop Thy still dews of quietness,
> Till all our striving cease;
> Take from our souls the strain and stress,
> And let our ordered lives confess
> The beauty of Thy peace.

So whether escaping for a weekend or napping for minutes, the leader finds his recreation in the union of a simple philosophy and strategic pauses.

No matter the pressure, leaders who arrive at their destination have learned the value of circlin' the wagons. They radiate a respect, a health, an energy, a peace. They are the select few who face reality with the resolution to keep recreating their strength.

When invited for the fifth time to address the NAWGA Prayer Breakfast, I revealed my heart to food executives who packed the dining room in this prayer which Pillsbury printed:

> Slow me down, Lord. . . .
> Slow the pounding of my racing pulse.
> May Your peace be a guarding army around my troubled mind.
> Do not let the complexities of computerized living be clouds that cover Your face for I choose to worship the Creator, not the creation.
> May your Spirit massage my tired muscles with the soothing ointment of faith and anoint my head with the revigorating oil of hope.
> Grant me the clarity to see truth . . . the courage to act honestly . . . the compassion to act fairly.

Amidst my prosperity give a value system that lets me prize the smile of my child, the thanksgiving of a warm meal, the blush of a picked rosebud, the purring of a kitten.

Let me always have an open hand of giving . . . the extended arm of cuddling . . . the sturdy shoulder of helping.

Give me enough stress to prevent distress.

Give me enough strength to overcome fear.

Give me enough sorrow to avoid arrogance.

Most of all, may people see my good works and glorify with me, my God who dwells within me.

And the wagon masters said, "Amen."

10

Sittin' Bull—
The Great Intimidator

Although he was credited with sixty coups, Sitting Bull, the great medicine man and leader of the Sioux nation in its final years, was not feared for his physical prowess in battle, as Crazy Horse, Red Cloud, and Gall were.

Sittin' Bull's real leadership power was spiritual. He claimed direct access to his nation's "Great Spirit" who spoke to him in visions and prophecies, some of which proved to be remarkably accurate.

Possessing a simple eloquence that often bordered on the poetic, he struck a deep chord in the hearts of all of his followers who considered him to be the embodiment of all that was Sioux or, indeed, Indian. For thirty years, from 1860 onward, both white man and Indian respected and feared his wily mind. General Custer underestimated him totally and paid for it with his life at the Little Big Horn. The United States and all of its politicians could not outnegotiate him. His end came at the hands not of a white man but of a fellow Sioux, as he had foretold in his dreams.

He was a deadly enemy possessed, it seemed, of superhuman powers. He knew that in the art of negotiation, after one's arguments are delivered, the first one who speaks—less than that, even blinks—loses the argument. Negotiation around the council fires was a serious game, for much was at stake and both sides had the men and power to enforce their decisions. He was a man who sorely tried men's souls.

Achievement Belongs to Those Who Persevere

The responsible leader blends character, intelligence, and perseverance. It is his responsibility to do so! Many are *ambitious to be leaders* but only a few become *ambitious leaders*. Interestingly, I have read books and heard lectures on building character and sharpening the intellect, but in my research I have found only one little book, printed long before I was born, on perseverance: *Plutarch's Lives*. Even when I used such synonyms as dynamism, desire, determination, persistence, or tenacity, pugnacity, or America's favorite—guts—I didn't find any exhaustive material. Yet isn't it fair to say that except for a few exceptions, achievement belongs to the person who perseveres?

Perseverance is the quality that Plutarch described as all-powerful: "Perseverance is the best friend and ally of those who use properly the opportunities that it presents, and the worst enemy of those who rush into action before it summons them."

It may be that "staring down Sittin' Bull" or perseverance is too demanding for the contemporary executive—and that's what I find disquieting about the contemporary books crossing my desk. One observer rightly has called the present phenomenon "management by the best seller" or, "the 20-minute daily exercises for being a success." Now a weekend retreat with a few lectures in the morning and recreation in the afternoon at an expensive, exotic spa is used to make leaders. We have learned how to condense in our lifetime, but I don't think we are about to reduce the thirty years Plato claimed necessary to develop a leader to thirty weeks.

Plutarch's masterpiece on leadership, which contains twenty-three biographies of notable Greeks and Romans, confirms this. Writing during the time of Nero, Plutarch brings great men and the events of their time into your study. He celebrates their lives as heroes, rather refreshing in our day when we overlook the leader's whole body to magnify the clay feet. From the lives of Alexander the Great, Fabius, Caesar, or some twenty others comes a strategy for today when continuity and consistency are being erased by expediency. Today even creativity is replaced by contrivance. Although leaders may vary in size and shape, Plutarch would have us note that they possessed on the positive side a perseverance which gave them the power to rise above negative intimidation.

Raw Versus Refined Pressure

It might be rudimentary, but tenacity alone, without definition and description, is insufficient. True perseverance is *refined*, for it incorporates character and intellect along with raw perseverance.

Let me give you a simple illustration of raw perseverance, first. In beautiful Berchtesgaden, Germany, I was completing a speaking engagement for the U.S. Air Force. A group of our generals and I were visiting in the foyer between the dining room and the kitchen. Out came a German waiter with a loaded tray. The waiter apparently believed that the shortest distance between two points is a straight line—a line which went right through the group of generals. Now most of our generals are great pals and effective leaders, but a few are persnickety and impressed with how many scrambled eggs they have had glued to their caps. I could see this type bristle as the waiter persistently marched through, splattering them on each side.

The Pentagon had briefed me before each of these tours that one of our functions was to better the U.S. image in the various nations where we had installations. Luckily, I realized we were about to have an "international incident" between the waiter and these generals, for even if the waiter didn't understand English, he could read body language and hear strong lungs exploding. So I tapped a couple of the generals on the arm and said, "Take comfort, fellows. That's why we won and they lost." They gracefully gave way.

During World War II if the Nazis were told to bomb Birmingham, England, their Prussian minds told them to go straight, even if every British antiaircraft gun was pointed their way, and then only one out of five of their bombers made it. Of course, the ill-fated four could go down in raw perseverance, shouting, "Glory to the Fuehrer."

Now, *refined* perseverance is more than the sheer display of energy found in raw perseverance. When we told the allied pilots to bomb Munich and keep Wernher von Braun off balance so he could not perfect the guided missiles, we allowed them some leeway. If met by defensive aircraft or ground guns, they could deviate and use their judgment to accomplish the mission.

To the old Prussian mind, I have no doubt I could say, "Go through the wall facing you," and he would do it; but using one's head as a battering ram would leave him so punchy on the other side that he would be totally ineffective. Others requested to go through a wall would walk down to the nearest exit, walk through and around and then tap the wall from the other side.

It isn't drive alone but direction that makes perseverance effective.

Unfortunately, I am afraid too many of our manufacturing firms, including such respected names as GM and USX, have depended too long on raw perseverance, throwing the power of resources at the problem instead of refining the intellect. Perseverance must outdistance personal ambition which acts only for today and not tomorrow.

Perseverance entails shrewdness but never sneakiness. Common sense is a basic component of wisdom. Wisdom is made up of judgment based on inquisitiveness, curiosity, experience, learning, and action. Wise perseverance is necessary because we no longer have the pillow for mistakes. The tearing down of the inflation curtain in the early 1980s took away the difficulties that cushioned ineffective leaders.

Alas, however, there is such a thing as "perseverance in error." Raw perseverance, which simply applies the heaviest thumb, caused Edmund Burke years ago to exclaim, "Perseverance is absurdity," and Samuel Taylor Coleridge to say, "Perseverance gives us a lantern on the stern which shines only on the water behind us."

Don't think for a moment I really support either/or. It's just that we have associated perseverance more with the physical than with the mental. Perseverance is brain and brawn joining together to address leadership opportunities. It is expressed both overtly and covertly: Overtly, in physical activity and energetic public appearance and covertly in reflection and reasoning. Covertly we generate the ideas that we overtly put into action.

Followers are fascinated and recruited by persevering leaders. Smartness, quickness, push, drive are their own magnets. Intelligent action always attracts attention to itself. In *Camping and Tramping with Roosevelt* (Boston: Houghton-Mifflin, 1907), John Burroughs wrote that Theodore Roosevelt was "doubtless the most vital man on the continent, if not on the planet, today."

Leadership perseverance gives one skills that appear effortless but are the result of practice. Horace Mann was described by his wife Mary as developing ". . . ingrained habits of work which became to him what water is to a fish." When he was asked how he achieved over and over again, Horace Mann characteristically replied: "In almost every case . . . it has required constant, hard, conscientious work. I consider there is no permanent success possible without hard and severe work, coupled with the highest and most praiseworthy aims."

Refined perseverance is using brawn and brain to fulfill the old adage, "Constant dripping wears away the hardest stone." Edward Bok in his day could have been prophetically viewing us today when he spoke of two infernal Americanisms: "That's good enough" and, "That will do." He said leaders arose from their peers because they were always busy perfecting their techniques. They never thought in terms of how little they could get away with but how much they could do. As President V. Raymond Edman used to counsel students at Wheaton College: "It is always too soon to quit."

As many of us desire to rise above shoddiness and sloppiness in our day, we can't do much better than go back to the Germanic thoroughness of Immanuel Kant:

> He was accustomed to view an argument from all points and in every possible light, to see whether it could stand the severest tests. This requires time; and haste in the solution of problems such as he investigated might have

175

proven fatal to his whole philosophy. His dread of error, and the earnest desire to make his position impregnable, made him slow and cautious.

So perseverance is not fools rushing in where angels fear to tread but deliberate action that leads to optimal achievement. Let me prepare you to meet the cowboys I will introduce to you—five who have stared down Sittin' Bull. Watch for these characteristics that they possess.

1. *The perseverers are able consistently to transcend their previous level of achievement.* They are unwilling to rest on their accomplished successes or those of their corporation.

2. *The perseverers believe there is not a "corporate comfort zone" and use the pauses in business not as a no man's land but as the staging ground for the next achievement.* They have a clear sense of their distinctive roles.

3. *The perseverers, guided by compelling internal goals, do not need external prodding nor will they be stopped by temporary detours.* They know where they will function and not function. They know what they will offer and not offer. They know what they should produce.

4. *The perseverers look at the worst-case scenario but are willing to take the risks justified by the worth of their goals.*

5. *The perseverers, when they fail, do not look somewhere to attach blame but for ways to turn the failure into a keystone for the next achievement.*

As perseverance becomes a lifestyle, so intimidation becomes a threat to our resolve. Sittin' Bull, that granite-looking, unmovable, legendary Indian chief of the West, is my way of humanizing intimidation. In the movies he was pictured as stepping out into the middle of a path and stopping a racing horse by simply holding up his hand. He could be sitting on his horse on the hill high above the battle and, with hardly a sound, control a battle like a puppeteer with a thousand strings. Sitting at the flap of his modest tent, he made it a palace where people entered and bowed in awe. Sittin' Bull was the Great Intimidator.

He Would Stare You Down

Nothing in his guttural sounds made a curriculum for psychoanalysis, but a psychologist he was. His silent stare was thundering.

The first person I would bring before the old chief to test his perseverance would be Jack Twyman.

If you are a "basketballer," you know Jack wears on his right hand his Hall of Fame ring, a tribute to his being All-Pro ten of eleven years that he played with the Cincinnati Royals (or Rochester Royals as they were called his first couple of years).

If you are a late-night TV movie addict, you might remember the movie about Jack and his devotion to injured teammate, Maurice Stokes, who fell after being mercilessly undercut by an opponent on the way to an easy "snowbird," never to arise again until his death a decade and a half later. You'd have been touched as you realized Jack and Maurice weren't pals, but were drawn by the question and the response of a warm heart to the ageless question, "If not me, who?" Maurice had no one but ancient parents with meager revenue, and he hadn't played long enough to salt much away. This was the era before rich signing bonuses and "Air Jordan" salaries.

In conservative Cincinnati, Jack legally made him Maurice Stokes Twyman, assuming full responsibility for nurses around the clock for twelve years. Each day he was home, Jack spent a few minutes at the hospital with Maurice. I was invited to give the dedicatory address for the field house bearing Maurice Stokes' name at his alma mater, St. Francis of Loretto. There was the Jonathan-David story of our time.

In the food business, as chairman and CEO of Super Food Services, Jack rapidly gained respect and attention as he led a shell of a company in fifteen years to become one of the most solid performers in the wholesale food business. He made all of us wish we had bought more stock.

Born a winner? Born a champ?

No, quite the opposite. We are not born winners or losers. In Jack's path was Sittin' Bull, and after a staring contest lasting three years, the old chief blinked.

Half a dozen years ago General Foods invited Jack to meet

with their key executives at New Jersey's Southbury Conference Center, strip himself of any false modesty, and share himself as they were trying to catch the intangible ingredient that makes an achiever. What he told them gave encouragement to the striver and erased any excuse from the rationalizer.

Jack told them that he had experienced three important events. He was cut from his high school basketball team three consecutive years: ninth, tenth, and eleventh grades. Cut three years in a row! When he went out the first year, the coach said, "You're going to be a pretty good size fellow, but you can't grow and run at the same time." That wasn't too hard to take. Very few make the varsity squad as freshmen.

In the tenth grade, Jack went out again. The coach responded this time, "Twyman, you're getting bigger—and slower." Put yourself back in that time. A coach had the role of a surrogate father. Not to measure up was to feel the world crumbling down on Atlas. Jack was like the great Disraeli hurrying his maiden speech before Parliament: "I sit down now, but the time will come when you will hear from me."

Most of us would have let well enough alone, but the next fall Jack was out for the team again. Now the coach had to reach up to wrap his arms around Jack's shoulders as he confidently advised: "Twyman, try golf. You're big enough to whack the ball a mile, and it doesn't take any speed to lope down the fairways!" Young people can be cruel to each other. Can't you imagine their snickers and taunting eyes as Jack's shoulders slumped and he wished he could disappear without having to walk out of the gym. To say the least, most of us would have finished our fling with basketball. Sittin' Bull would have won!

Instead, at that moment, Jack decided he was going to play varsity basketball his senior year. Matthew, a Christian Brother teacher at Pittsburgh Central Catholic, saw Jack's disappointment but also recognized his resolve. He found some other fellows cut from the squad and formed a team he called the Apaches.

There is a strange law: Strong resolution always attracts unknown resources.

These young men played every industrial team that would schedule them, playing as many as three or four games a week. Finally in March they played the varsity and won. Jack had proven that what you—not others—can believe about yourself, you can with singleness of purpose achieve. He would not let any person, even his coach, act as judge of his life. As Charles Buxton wrote, "Experience shows that sometimes success is due less to ability than zeal. The winner is he who gives himself to his work . . . body and soul."

Now the coach *had* to let Jack suit up his senior year; and in only one year, this sixteen-year-old did what no other had; he became All-State. He received one college scholarship offer from the University of Cincinnati where he became All-American. The rest, including the Hall of Fame, is history. Upon retirement he gave direction to the insurance company that he started while he was in college. He knew an achievement is never final but rather the door for another opportunity. You may have become better acquainted with Jack as color commentator on ABC's *Game of the Week*. He covered the summer Olympics in Mexico City.

It was my honor as a new board member at Super Foods to smell financial trouble, as only a long Phoenician nose can smell, and I made the motion for Jack to replace the existing chairman. His election was the rebirth of a fine corporation. Jack has proven that the stumbling blocks you climb over in one struggle become the stepping stones for the next challenge.

If you are a cynic, you might contend that Jack didn't so much rise above intimidation as escape his honorable but less than prosperous Sacramento Street neighborhood of Pittsburgh. What did he have to lose? Basketball was his ticket out, no matter how illusive. Whatever the reason, he "stared down" Sittin' Bull and made him blink.

What Is True Worth?

Now let's go across the tracks and visit with J. Harriss Covington who had just as much challenge to break shackles although by all appearances he "had it made!"

Life begins at forty, but for "Cov" forty produced just the opposite feeling. He had the appearance of success and control to everyone but himself. He had the credentials: "prepping" at Woodberry Forest, graduating from Princeton, distinguished Naval service, proper marriage to his lovely Helen, two sons and a daughter, executive of his own prosperous hosiery firm, only heir to the estates of both his mother and an unmarried uncle, consistently successful civic leader, membership in the best circles, and on and on.

Yes, this was the man who called me to the privacy of his home to tell me he was intimidated by the whole world. Facing Sittin' Bull, he was hanging his head. In fact, he was going to the University of North Carolina Hospital and staying under psychiatric guidance until he solved the riddle.

Friends don't like that. You are not supposed to admit to neurotic thoughts, personal hang-ups, or inner insecurities. You are never to wrestle with self-concept or question your competence. It is irrational for a handsome, debonair gentleman to be fearful or depressed or withdrawn. Such behavior indicts the whole system. Physical agony brings out sympathy in us. Mental anxiety tends to disgust us. We reach out to troubled souls, but we turn away from troubled minds. We can not understand Dr. O. Hobart Mowrer who distinguished himself by being elected president of the American Psychological Association only to be too depressed to attend his own installation.

So in my city it was a troubled Sunday school class at our most proper church that received a letter from Harriss informing them he would be at Chapel Hill Hospital until he "saw the sun come up again." Our friendship took a new depth as I wrote him at the hospital to commend him for facing God and asking for help to face himself and thus starting to move beyond intimidation. It was not an easy valley to climb out of. Harriss was fathered by a genius who had come to town and married its most desirable debutante. Harriss' father could do no wrong in business and had only one apparent weakness, excessive drinking. Divorce in a small southern city was anathema then, but the weakness of drink drove Harriss' *parents* to split. It was the child who felt rejected and became the subject of community false pity. The separation was so complete that Harriss was denied even a picture of his father.

Now, years later, he felt a double whammy. Had his father left some genetic weakness in him? Had Harriss abandoned his father to the social wolves to die alone, almost destitute? Neither problem was real, nor could Harriss be accountable for action taken by parents while he was still a child. Anxiety is never repelled by simple logic, however Harriss had to see himself as a worthy individual when stripped of all the social trappings and proper surroundings. Persevering through a year and a half of intensive therapy and with the help of his analyst, he determined the cause of his depression and resolved it. Upon bringing the trauma of his childhood to the surface, life took on new meaning.

As Jack Twyman found his worth amidst "put-downs," Harriss Covington had to find himself amidst "put-ups." One had to outstare criticism; the other, compliments. Criticism and compliments can be equally damaging.

The steps to outstare this Sittin' Bull include:

1. *Concentration on personal values as opposed to community agenda.* We often say our friends are the last to tell us. Actually, our problem is deciding who are really friends. We have built-in social mediocrity. As Jack was not to accept the coach's judgment as final and give up on basketball, Harriss was not to question his "life of privilege." Real spirituality begins with questions of who we are. The pilgrim who makes progress goes to the doubter's castle first.

2. *Confidence in one's own abilities based on realistic evaluation.* We may emulate others, but we come home to ourselves. Dreams may be necessary for growth, but we need to discern when they are shelters from reality and excuses for laziness. Laziness in this instance has no relationship to activity. Activity is not accomplishment. Confidence comes to the person who vigorously sees obstacles as stimuli.

3. *Service to others defines oneself better than a mirror can.* Like Jack in his service to Maurice Stokes, Harriss saw his children not as an extension of a social image but as three distinctive individuals to guide at their different paces and needs. Fellow sufferers have benefitted, for Harriss believes we know best what we've experienced and the way to be healed is in using your pain to help others.

181

Sittin' Bull Would Surround You

If the stare of Sittin' Bull doesn't wilt you, the backdrop of hundreds and hundreds of Indians staring certainly can create insufferable odds.

What do you do when you have just reported the best record in your century-old business? For the company's annual meeting, you have taken the board of directors to the site of your newest and biggest acquisition, and the applause is still ringing in your ears when the next morning you are awakened by the news that your stock has been secretly purchased by a corporate raider who awaits your surrender. That is where Ted Wetterau of Wetterau Incorporated, the third largest food wholesaler in the United States, found himself on August 19, 1981.

At first, this Sittin' Bull, a propane distributor from the Midwest, did not seem particularly menacing. But it was quickly discovered that the raider sat on takeover king Victor Posner's board, that this was his fourth unfriendly tender offer, and that he had nearly unlimited financial support from Continental Illinois Bank and several others. These included an honorable organization, Security Pacific National Bank, which unwittingly had supported Continental but withdrew as soon as they learned the intended use of the credit line.

Continental's charter also precluded loans for unfriendly tender offers during this period, but Wetterau's trauma occurred under the old regime before they were humbled by near collapse and were rescued only by extraordinary actions by the Federal banking system. At the time a $100-million line of credit could be authorized with impunity by a junior officer as long as the borrower had the words *gas* or *oil* in the company name. Unfortunately, this borrower qualified in that regard, and as a result, a spotty balance sheet and negative cash flow were ignored. Also ignored was the raider's reputation for questionable business practices that had led a federal judge to characterize the raider's actions as an attempt to loot the assets of an earlier takeover target. Dozens of articles painted a grim picture in Kansas City newspapers.

This attack was no feint by a roving band of renegades. This was war. Ted recognized the challenge and answered it by forming a small response team of company officers and out-side experts and calling together the directors for con-sultation. This was typical of Wetterau under Ted's guidance, no sound and fury, action instead.

It was quickly apparent that the odds were against survival. *The Wall Street Journal* had reported that between 85 and 90 percent of all unfriendly takeover attempts succeeded. The response team laid out the options they could recommend: accept the offer; reject the offer and begin a legal battle; seek an alternative offer from a "white knight." In view of their opin-ion of the raider, the directors selected the last two alter-natives.

With the announcement, the quiet suburban headquarters of Wetterau exploded with activity. This was now a first-class television story; camera crews and announcers clamored for the definitive story. This was an arbitrage play; phones rang continuously. The pressure began to build.

To understand the reaction of a man to a crisis, it is useful to know what has come before to mold his character. Ted was the youngest of the Wetterau clan when he left his study for the ministry to join the company. He did so at the request of his father. It would not be the last time that he put his family's interests ahead of his own.

When he arrived on the scene, the leadership of the com-pany included his father, Ted, his uncle, Otto, and his much older cousin, Ollie. Company sales were $23 million. The company was narrowly defined as a wholesale grocer, and to Ted its prospects for growth looked limited.

He buckled down to the tasks assigned; sifting tons of flour was one he would never forget. He also studied hard and became a journeyman meat cutter. But no matter what en-gaged his body, his mind dreamed of a new definition of Wetterau, a definition that included providing the services that an independent retailer needed to become successful.

After a year he felt the frustration that overwhelms all creative young men. No one would listen. No one would risk change. He decided that the only way to build credibility was to become a retailer himself. Leaving Wetterau Incorporated he took his modest savings and joined a long-time friend in the ownership of a small IGA market.

For the next two years he had three objectives: to build a successful business; learn all he could about retailing; and identify the true needs of a retailer. He did all three as he worked seventy to eighty hours a week. He found he was a natural marketeer. He visited every housewife within a two-mile radius and invited them to shop his store. As a result of this and other activities, the volume of the store doubled in two years.

Once more, his father asked him to join the company. This time he agreed—but only if he could begin to make changes.

Each year in January the executives met to consider plans for the coming year. Ted spent the time between Christmas and New Year's Day writing proposals and reviewing them with his wife Helen, very much a member of his team.

Ted envisioned a full service organization that provided for the retailer needs he had identified. He felt the company should be able to design and build stores, provide for retailers' accounting needs, act as merchandising consultants, provide nonfood items, and so on. This was the first vision of the role of a modern wholesaler. He also felt that the company should position itself to grow explosively. He saw in the future $1 billion in sales. The board listened to his plans each year and rejected them. He did not give up and at last he made progress. He was permitted to acquire a construction company. As head of store development, a new department, he created a modularized store concept, called a "package" store that brought him worldwide attention. In 1961 he led a drive to take the company public, and the modern era of Wetterau began. Incidentally, his dream had been to reach $1 billion in sales by 1980. He made it in 1979.

He reached his dream and now faced a nightmare.

Faced with an enormously complex problem, a hostile force, Ted once more felt the family presence. This time the heritage and sacrifice of 112 years and four generations pressed down upon him. His father, Uncle Otto, and Cousin Ollie had long since passed on, but a new generation, his own children, had been added.

The company had gone public in 1961, and the Wetterau family no longer owned the majority of its stock, but the generations of leadership made the burden just as great and the frustration even more daunting. Against this backdrop, Ted turned to his two greatest sources of inspiration and strength, his religion and his immediate family. A deeply religious man who never flaunted his faith, Ted's principal manifestation of deep conviction was his practice of starting every board meeting with a prayer. Each emergency meeting during this period began with a prayer for guidance and strength.

I am convinced that he received both. Ted tells me that twice during and once soon after the crisis, he went against all advice and simple logic to make decisions. In all three cases, he felt compelled to turn down the best advice available and proceed on a different course.

In two cases the logical choice might have led to major ownership positions by foreign companies and the third logical choice would have led to an acquisition that could have brought down a weakened Wetterau after the fight was over.

The other factor that kept him in the fight was the support and conviction of his own family, Helen, an ardent and able supporter and wife, sons Conrad and Mark, and daughter Beth.

Obviously, Ted could have blinked when faced with overwhelming odds. He and this loving family could have been wealthy beyond most men's dreams if only they had taken the raider's offer. Ted knew, however, that not all of his shareholders would get the same offer and that some would surely be cheated if the company was torn apart for profit. This was the subject of the family meeting that convinced Ted he must not only fight on, but win despite the risks. His children told him, "Dad, we aren't concerned about the business for ourselves. Who knows if we'll even become a part of the company? But, there are more than four thousand people who work for the company and thousands of shareholders who will suffer if we give in to this threat." That night Helen and Ted shared their usual prayer time, and the decision was made.

Was it the right decision? After the confrontation was past, says Dick Dalton, senior vice president, sales stood at nearly $2 billion, but net earnings had fallen to less than $2 million, total assets were $327 million and Wetterau's common stock was selling as low as $10⅝. However, the battle seemed to strengthen not only the management team, but the company as a whole. Wetterau reacted as if it had been tempered by flame. Although some in financial circles bet the company could never recover, in five years it was a company of twelve thousand employees, almost $4 billion in sales, with eighteen times the earnings, twice the assets, and a healthy stock that was selling in the mid $40s.

Ted Wetterau rose to meet the challenge, and his team, including the directors, proved worthy of the trial. But he, like Sittin' Bull who attributed his strength to the Great Spirit, feels his success and strength were derived from faith and a gift from God.

So many of the successful people I know take no pride unto themselves and deflect all praise to the Lord. In Ted's case, he had fought hard battles all of his life and this became another test of his will and vision.

Ted Wetterau would now give a hearty *amen* to these questions and answers from B.C. Forbes fifty years ago.

> Do difficulties depress you or brace you up? If you stop to think of it, wouldn't life become monotonous, colorless, deadening were we to cease to have to battle against obstacles? Difficulties should act as a tonic. They should spur us to greater exertion. I honestly think that difficulties, like work, are blessings in disguise, and that if we would study this subject through to the bottom, we would arrive at this conclusion.

When Sittin' Bull and his tribe surround us, we normally:

1. *Experience fear.* The unexpected usually has us catching our breath. No disease is as threatening to the psyche of the achiever as the fear of failure.

2. *Consider surrendering, but as we think about what we surrender, we should be counting our strengths.* The inventory of what we would give up reinforces what we have.

3. *Feel gratitude.* Gratitude opens our eyes not only to what we are saving but to what we should be. Gratitude has three effects: a) Gratitude readjusts our focus. We sense that our employees aren't any more dependent on us than we are on

them. Their trust in us enhances our self-worth if we don't fail them. We move from subjective to objective. b) Gratitude reinforces our serenity. By thanking someone we are realizing we're not islands. Help is available if we reach out. c) Gratitude releases our feelings. The tendency toward paranoia is replaced by openness.

Sittin' Bull and Friends Do Have Arrows

Sittin' Bull and our hero at the Saturday matinee have reached an impasse! With a gesture of the chief's hand, the braves form a circle, and now the outcome of any confrontation between the cowboys and the Indians will depend on our hero's defending his honor fighting Sittin' Bull's selection of "the bravest of his braves." As our hero is strippin' down for wrestling, a "bow-happy" warrior fires, the arrow lodging in the shoulder of our hero. Fight's over before it begins—or is it? You can still remember our cowboy knowing he can't pull it, reaching over, snapping off the shaft and moving to the center of the ring to commence the fight. For just a "flick of a moment" admiration crosses the stoical face of Sittin' Bull.

So there is a special category of leadership for the persons taking blows in stride and rising above what others call handicaps. Years ago, I remember Dr. W. A. Criswell preaching a sermon with a premise that "handicaps are the compliment of God. You only handicap thoroughbreds." The mystic St. Theresa of Avila also observed centuries ago that deprivations of good health are God's signature of His favor.

Such is the untold story of Sam Walton. On the eve of the day that Sam Walton would explode on the pages of the business press (triggered primarily by Forbes' questionable "wealth-o-meter"), Sam and Helen Walton were adjusting to his confirmed leukemia. If the stock analysts were concerned about succession at Wal-Mart stores under normal conditions, think how they would have run for cover had they known the real story.

Sam Walton had joined the late Albert Schweitzer's exclusive "Fellowship of Those Who Bear the Mark of Pain," reserved for those who have bodily impairment or mental stress or emotional strain. Such people as James W. Angell wrote about in *Yes Is a World* (Waco: Word Books, 1974): "Life derives some of its shine from the fact that it takes so much guts to cope with it."

Sam Walton's Wal-Mart stores were a going reality, when Wetterau Incorporated approached him with a unique proposition. Wetterau had a group of discount stores called MohrValu that was teaching them that they should stay in the food business. Executive Vice President Jack Ryan of Wetterau was dispatched to see if Sam Walton would buy them. At that time Sam built his units one by one, but this group deal was intriguing. He wanted all the discount stores but two, which he thought were way too large for his plans. Jack set a price based on total sale. After more negotiations, Sam bought all the stores, the only group he has ever bought, and they became his quantum leap forward. The two stores "too big" became his standard size.

It was one success on top of another, but even a billionaire can't fix the diagnosis when his doctor in Tulsa says, "leukemia." While others might have been thrown into depression, Sam echoed the words of Evgraf in *Dr. Zhivago*: "And remember you must never, under any circumstances, ultimately despair." He just wouldn't accept that he had a terminal illness. The famed M. D. Anderson Medical Center was chosen for further diagnosis. After eighteen months of treatment, there was still no sense of finality. Sam kept right on his schedule of opening stores and increasing business. He could well accept Grace Crowell's prayer from her months of bed confinement:

> Lord, make me brave for life, braver
> than this.
> Help me to straighten after pain,
> As the tree straightens after the rain,
> Smiling and shining again.

Those rare people who break off the arrow and keep moving have learned and practiced three lessons.

Walton Lesson 1: Life is finite and has limitations. For Sam and his wife, Helen, their loving marriage means they are best friends and full partners in all phases of their life. They remind me of what Pat Brown told me years ago. Pat, it seemed, was destined for failure. As a teenager he lost a leg. All the medical profession had as replacement was a glorified "peg leg." Pat was big and heard the taunts of his classmates. In the Depression, he went bankrupt with a Ford agency and nearly drowned in a sea of debts. He rose from the quagmire to pay off each creditor with 6 percent interest (not bad for the 1930s) and then built a lumber empire. For years we attended the home football games at Chapel Hill together, and I was curious about how he survived: "Tom, if you can have one person who believes totally in you and if you are fortunate enough that this one person is your wife, you can come back again—and again—and still again," replied Pat.

Sam has that. In fact, three or four years earlier, he had faced Helen's cancer, and they decided they would accept it but not surrender to it. She would be a total mother for their children and be at Sam's side each step of the way. The Walton's didn't know my "guru," Norman Cousins, but they are further proof of what Norman teaches to doctors at UCLA—that attitude can trigger your immune system. You remember that Norman Cousins has been designated for death three times but has refused to go! In the finest sense, the Waltons learned to face life with humor—one day at a time. Ben Franklin's *Poor Richard's Almanac* has the line: "Trouble knocked at the door but, hearing a laugh, hurried away."

President Jack Kennedy once sent a friend a silver beer mug with the inscription: "There are three things which are real: God, human folly, and laughter. The first two are beyond comprehension. So we must do what we can with the third." Or to put it in scriptural perspective, the wise King Solomon would tell us in Ecclesiastes, "Gladness of the heart is the life of a man and the joyfulness of a man prolongeth his days"; or as Proverbs says, "A merry heart does good like medicine, But a broken spirit dries the bones."

You can't fake that everything is okay. That would be white-washing a rotting fence, but you can take each day as a gift. Harriet Caldwell of Chattanooga demonstrated this. When Duke Hospital said, "No hope," she and her husband Hard-wick decided how they would enjoy each day. The arrow of death was just a reminder of finiteness of human beings but not her destroyer. She well knew that all of us have a deadline.

Sam and Helen, knowing they were finite, took the sting out of a dramatic arrow as soon as it pierced them.

Walton Lesson 2: Being finite doesn't excuse us from doing something infinite. They accepted the responsibility that Longfellow suggested in his "A Psalm of Life":

> We can make our lives sublime,
> And, departing, leave behind us
> Footprints on the sands of time.

That doesn't suggest that knowing you are finite makes you seek to do the dramatic each day. You just go on living your normal routine but separating chaff from the kernel. Sam had always lived on the cutting edge. His parents had difficulty in the Depression. Sam's dad was unemployed for a while and then had only modest income as a Metropolitan insurance man going door to door to people with no money for weekly premiums. Instead of feeling sorry for himself, he became more aggressive. This attracted Helen to him and to her dad. Helen's father was a lawyer and businessman who, seeing a good idea, was willing to borrow against all of his assets with no worry, feeling it was necessary in order to achieve what he wanted for his family.

He encouraged his new son-in-law even when Sam owed $1.5 million. Sam paid off that debt by selling his Ben Franklin store. He moved to Bentonville, Arkansas, and plunged right back into things again. There didn't seem to be any other way.

His strategy? He and Helen carefully screened the people they hired. They wanted people who delivered papers, milked cows, worked in stores after school, attended church regularly. They believed, as I do, that people with good work and worship habits usually manage their time efficiently. They looked for both good work and humble worship.

These are the people he rallied in staff meetings each week when he was small and whom he now visits in his scattered retail empire. Helen says she is still amazed at the energy that Sam generates when he talks before employees and shares Wal-Mart dreams.

If you read the biographies, you might think Sam is all work. He can relax. He can stop everything and play a "wicked" game of tennis with no thought of losing. Nothing interferes or interrupts his daily hunts during bird season. He can still romp with his grandchildren.

Sam is surprisingly reflective. What was it a famous anthropologist wrote comparing East and West? The Western mind says, "Don't just stand there; do something." The West is action-oriented. The Eastern mind says, "Don't do anything; stand there." The Eastern mind is attuned to contemplation. Achiever leaders, like Sam, balance action and contemplation. They take time to dream so they know what to fulfill.

Walton Lesson 3: The arrow makes you review your battle plan and adjust. Cancer, emotional distress, external attacks, economic upheavals—all are ugly phenomena which can't be denied. Yet once we accept them as real and identify them as the enemy, we can outline our battle plan.

The only fatal enemy is not accepting yourself and life's fortunes.

John Steinbeck wrote:

> Most people do not like themselves at all. They distress themselves, put on masks and pomposities. They quarrel and boast and pretend and are jealous because they do not like themselves. If we could learn to like ourselves even a little, maybe our cruelties and angers might melt away. Maybe we would not have to hurt one another just to keep our ego chins above water.

The real test is not the arrow from without but the attitude from within. If we take it objectively and not subjectively, all the arrow does is focus our challenge.

Peter Drucker says, "Whenever anything is being accomplished, it is being done, I have learned, by a monomaniac with a mission." Leaders aren't casual. "Fanatacism is crucial." A recent study of Nobel prize winners found them to have peasant toughness, a streak of intolerance, a killer instinct, yet a sense of humor. They are strong finishers.

The arrow doesn't change the direction of the leader; it only helps him rediscover the value of life before achieving great leadership. Just a couple of years ago Bill Marriott, Jr., had reached a high plateau. The hotels were doing well. He was the darling of the service industry. He had his new properties in Atlanta, Washington, and New York City. Starting the engine of his boat at his family lake resort in New Hampshire, Bill was literally blown out of the water, destined to bear scars for life. Did he stop? No, he accelerated. All it did was send him back to what his father had written to him. It was 1964; Bill was in his early thirties.

Willard Marriott, Sr., called "a living example of the American dream" by President Reagan, was wrestling with the leadership of the corporation he and his wife had started as a nine-seat root beer stand in Washington, D.C. On the day of the announcement that Willard was naming his son president, he penned this note of personal advice:

1. Keep physically fit, mentally and spiritually strong.
2. Guard your habits—bad ones will destroy you.
3. Pray about every difficult problem.
4. Study and follow professional management principles.
5. People are No. 1—their development, loyalty, interest, team spirit. Develop managers in every area.
6. Decisions: People grow making decisions and assuming responsibility for them.
   • Make crystal clear what decision each manager is responsible for and what decisions you reserve for yourself.
   • Have all the facts and counsel necessary—then decide and stick to it.
7. Criticism: Don't criticize people but make a fair appraisal of their qualifications with their supervisor only (or someone assigned to do this).
8. See the good in people and try to develop those qualities.
9. Inefficiency: If it cannot be overcome and an employee is obviously incapable of the job, find a job he can do or terminate *now.* Don't wait.

10. Manage your time.
- Short conversations—to the point.
- Make every minute on the job count.
- Work fewer hours—some of us waste half of our time.

11. Delegate and hold accountable for results.

12. Details:
- Let your staff take care of them.
- Save your energy for planning, thinking, working with department heads, promoting new ideas.
- Don't do anything someone else can do for you.

13. Ideas and competition:
- Ideas keep the business alive.
- Know what your competitors are doing and planning.
- Encourage all management to think about better ways and give suggestions on anything that will improve business.
- Spend time and money on research and development.

14. Don't try to do an employee's job for him—counsel and suggest.

15. Think objectively and keep a sense of humor. Make the business fun for you and others.

After the boating accident, Bill didn't change his course but, like Sam Walton, just decided to do it even better. Ironically, when struck by the arrow, one doesn't seek more days in his life but more life in his days. Arrows give us life's true perspective.

I remember the story of the new member of British Parliament who brought his eight-year-old daughter to tour London. Visiting Westminster Abbey, she seemed awestruck by the size and beauty of the magnificent structure. Her beaming dad, wondering what was going on in her mind, asked, "And what, my child, are you thinking about at this moment?"

She answered, "Daddy, I was thinking how big you are in our house but how small you look here!"

Out of the mouths of children, right? So the arrow reminding us of the finite makes us all the more grateful for the leadership privilege for however long it may last.

So Sittin' Bull is faced by all of us. Our leadership is freed and useful to the degree we rise above intimidation. In this chapter we have seen that we have some options.

We can accept the rejection or defeat as final from the stare to the arrow. This will lead to pathological feelings of uselessness and finding ourselves feeling sorry for ourselves so we act with disorganization and degeneration.

We can act as if we are not intimidated. We can deny the attack, trying to buy time, believing time alone will give us another chance to change the environment.

We can redouble our energy and turn our disadvantage into advantage. We defy the opposition by hustle and the inspired focalization of our energies so even our modest talents effectively defeat genius.

We can find spiritual reserves that are never sensed till by default we call upon them. Humor and courage blend into poise. We take risks we feared before, but our awareness of finitude really says, "What can I lose?" so we reach achievements that never could have been without defeats.

11

They Came to Stay

Out of the whole panoply of adventurers who roamed the West only a few really came to stay. The early mountain men, for instance, were really seeking just beaver furs. When the beaver hat went out of fashion in 1840, the mountain man switched to guiding the pioneers. When the great guides like Kit Carson and Jedediah Smith were no longer needed, they settled for running the local trading posts.

When the gold rush of 1849 came, almost a million people joined it. But when the lodes played out they returned to the East. The famed gunslingers and gamblers preyed on their hosts only until the preacher, the law, and the school marm crossed the Platte.

The noble red man and the U. S. Cavalry who chased them left little but rudiments of forts and headstones.

It fell to the pioneers, ranchers, and farmers, men and women who came to stay, to develop and build lasting worth in this new land. They did not achieve their goals in a season, a year, or a decade. The great families of the West, like the Kings, Stuarts, and Kennedys from Texas to Montana, Kansas City to California, spent a generation of labor to build their value. In the process they brought civilization to the plains. They knew that nature yields slowly to the hand of man, but yield it does.

The Two Types of Business Leaders

I divide the heads of business into two general groups: first, the movers and shakers; and secondly, the builders and stayers. Sometimes in the past they overlapped and were even synonymous, but not today. At precise moments there is a need for the mover and shaker, the hired, quick-draw lawman who runs the renegade hombres out of town. But the frontier town soon learned that the trigger-happy badgeman was useful only for a short time.

The communities of the Old West, not unlike corporations today, were built by those who came to stay. With a personal commitment and investment they balanced power with prudence, ambition with accommodation, strength with steadiness. It is my contention that the impatient and impetuous, whom we may admire in the short term, invariably come out indifferent and inconsiderate in the long term. We might accept slow finishers as the price we must pay for a fast start, but too often today in corporate life we have the "no-finishers." The instant heroes leave in their wake the mergers, the acquisitions, the job losses, the home disruptions, the empty office buildings, the weed-choked factory yards, the erasure of corporate names and products. The rush for mandated benefits, that harm the very employees they propose to help, will become law because of the support of bludgeoned unemployed middle managers who are casualties of the "mover and shaker."

While seeking to uncover the difference between those with staying power and the fast-deal artists, I discovered that those with staying power have a respect for history accompanied by a sense of destiny. The people who give leadership are not single-dimension individuals but have a rich variety of interests and personal qualities. I will describe several of these characteristics of a leader with staying power.

SOUL OF AN ARTIST

Without question our Western pilgrims chose their homestead cities for water access, wind swirls, a place easy to protect, the richness of the soil, the size of the potential spread, accessibility to neighbors, the sun rays. Yet as we revisit those early homeplaces or frontier towns, we are impressed that while staking out for survival, they didn't forget the aesthetics. They realized it takes more than four walls and a room to make a dwelling livable and were grateful for the piece of art or heirloom they had sneaked onto the wagon.

The "soul of an artist" could be found in those rugged early westerners just as outer hand-sewn garments have no relationship to the inner person. Unfortunately, we have made the soul of the artist synonymous with softness, disorganization, and freewheeling spirit.

"Soul of an artist" means you can discern between the temporal and the lasting. We have grown up being taught that businessmen are rapacious, and we rarely learn about the business-statesmen like Andrew Carnegie and John Wanamaker who today are recognized as possessing the soul of the artist.

John Bryan, the chairman of Sara Lee, is systematic, organized, disciplined, tough, and dynamic with a cautious flair. And he has an artist's soul. His college studies were not in the arts but economics and business administration. His artist soul simply colored the way he would apply business tactics when he returned to Mississippi at age twenty three to take over the family business.

Art's idealism, openness, and freedom of expression force one to ask impertinent questions about the sacrosanct. Jacob Bronowski, physicist and artist, said, "Until you ask an impertinent question of nature, you do not get a pertinent answer." The questions that are asked really give us the solutions that have changed our society.

Art allows us to trust our hunches and our gut reactions. While the technocrats depend solely on the facts to make their decisions, the artist depends on his emotions. In contemporary business today we rely too heavily on rationality and not enough on emotions.

Art is expression for our emotions and is really an emotional expression of philosophy, religion, morals, and ethics. Art not only reveals the artist's agony or ecstasy but by reducing the emotions to a canvas lets us see problems or pleasures as manageable. Art demands that we empathize and sympathize while still giving us an escape, letting us move into ancient or new worlds where we haven't been but can dream.

From the security John Bryan found in the permanence of art, he took the courage to challenge his business. If an institution or corporation can't be questioned, it doesn't deserve to survive. Making money for shareholders short term was routine but he wanted to grow long term. John once said, "I know how to make money, but there is much more to life than financial concerns."

The artistic, emotional approach allows for holistic thinking. Believing that art, to be art, has to have form and color and organization is the basis of how John Bryan has built Sara Lee. The old Consolidated Company he took over was really without form, like artist's material. It was pieces, a piece of marble here, a flower there, red paint somewhere else. Dissimilar companies are not a problem, but dissimilar companies without a common tie ignored their corporate relationship. He separated the waste companies from the valued. He built a small but extremely capable corporate staff, carefully hand-picking the people. He trusted; he delegated; he was candid; he rewarded them before their peers for achieving results; he stroked the discouraged and kept himself alert with tidy memos. The company now had form. Organization was becoming evident as the companies, still dissimilar, complemented each other and gave enough collective strength to move slowly but deliberately into the international scene.

Color was added to the form and organization when he covered the nondescript "Consolidated" name with the bright colorful "Sara Lee." John feels it encumbent to keep Sara Lee simple, for simplicity is the essence of truth. Keats' famous line, "Beauty is truth, truth beauty," strikes me as I visit Sara Lee.

Do you enjoy irony? Then visit the company that makes large profits from grinding sausage, selling hosiery packed in "half goose eggs," and owning one of the nation's most significant art collections. If you visit Sara Lee in the First National Tower in downtown Chicago, you enter a fresh but nondescript office building, not unlike dozens in metropolitan

America. The sameness ends when you enter the offices of Sara Lee. You are met at the elevator entrance by the seven-foot bronze *Upright Motion* by Henry Moore. The reception area wall is graced with the very large painting by Édouard Vuillard, *Public Garden*. At the ends of hallways to the right and left are *The Bathers* by Roger de la Fresnaye, and *The Apple Pickers* by Pierre Bonnard. Down the center hallway is Fernand Léger's abstract *Still Life with Compass*. In every hall, office, or lobby the walls are replete with master artworks from Toulouse-Lautrec to Degas.

So what? Didn't John inherit one of the great corporate art collections assembled by his predecessors and self-described mentor, Nathan Cummings? Yes, in Nate existed the desire for the accumulation of art, but in John is the soul of the artist.

John Bryan, whether on the phone or in person, belies the massive responsibility he bears. He seems unbusy. He doesn't allow himself to be rushed. Reading Daniel Dancocks's *Sir Arthur Currie* (New York: Methuen), Canada's great general of World War I who later became principal and vice-chancellor of McGill University, I found these lines that made me think of John: "No visitor could fail to be struck with two things at General Currie's headquarters," observed war correspondent Fred Mackenzie. He continued:

> The first was the air of quiet and calm that surround the man. There was no feverish rush . . . things were so organized . . . that routine matters were dealt with by routine men and the commander was left free to think out the real decisions. You might at first even receive the impression of leisure. But when you know the commander better, you would discover that your appointment has been carefully fitted in among others, that conference and review, interview and parade, and conference again followed one another in unceasing succession from early morning till late at night.

But John is also disciplined, and his views on discipline are simple. Discipline is the self-control that guides us in doing the right thing in any given situation. Only his perfectionist nature reveals a slight tenseness.

John Bryan believes that "a business is nothing but a collection of people." Thus the corporation is to be a major player in every aspect of community life. He feels we have allowed the public square to become, in the term of Richard Neuhaus, "naked." We have allowed our social and corporate institutions to drift away from their moorings. We have ceased being clear about the standards we hold forth and the principles by which we judge. If we are clear in our minds, we have done too little to impact the public. He goes a step further and believes the corporation should be held responsible for contemporary life. He simply believes we can always make things better, and he just doesn't back off.

John translates hopes to practical dimensions, so he, as much as any one person, brought about the tax reform of 1986. Why? To save money for himself, Sara Lee, the food industry? No. It was not a modest issue. He saw tax reform as unshackling middle America. He found the present tax encroachment a stifler of creativity, a diminisher of energy, a frustrater of dreams. As passed, the legislation looks a bit like Swiss cheese but is still a sound movement in the right direction. The price of passage left scars on John, but people with healthy philosophies have historically been among the first to enter the pragmatic foxholes of the firing line.

VERSATILITY

The early settler was forced by the circumstances to be a person for all seasons. He had to be equally enthusiastic as a father, designer, homemaker, builder, rancher, farmer, defender, lawman. If a leader must have character and wisdom, he must also have energy to perform. Yes, energy is essential to leadership. Skill that looks effortless is the result of steady energy. Spasmodic effort, no matter how strong, has limited value. Consistency, continuity, and caring are the keys. One source for this energy is versatility. Unlike the "pop-advisors" who recommend narrow goals sought with singular effort at a frenzied pace, the true leader is multidimensional. Versatility is the mark of distinction. The experience of one facet of his life is applied to the others. Isn't that the way it has always been with leaders? Michelangelo excelled in painting, music, sculpture, engineering. David Starr Jordan was recognized in ichthyology, geology, biology, religion, government, university administration, and international affairs. Teddy Roosevelt made his mark as a naturalist, general, president, writer, lecturer. John Burroughs said of him, "He is many-sided, and every side throbs with his tremendous life and energy; the pressure is equal all around" (*Camping and Training with Roosevelt*). Maybe never has history recorded another like Leonardo da Vinci. The world still reveres his paintings and drawings, his sculpture, his designs, his inventions. His creations go from *The Last Supper* to the wheelbarrow and include the flexible roller chain, paddle wheel, armored car, spring motor-driven car, camera, telescope, marble-cutting machine, concave mirror, diving suit, and flying machine.

Versatility not only keeps the John Bryans from monotony but one skill also becomes the energy source for the next. Norman Cousins reported his visit to Albert Schweitzer in Lambaréné. The day had been tedious at the hospital. An ordinary person would be ready to collapse. Dr. Cousins wrote:

> Late that evening, after most of the oil lamps at the hospital had been turned out, I walked down toward the compound. From the direction of Dr. Schweitzer's quarters, I could hear the stately progression of a Bach toccata. The Doctor was playing on the piano in his small workroom. . . . I went up on the porch and stood for perhaps five minutes near the latticed window, through which I could see Dr. Schweitzer's silhouette in the dim-lighted room. Then there was a pause in the music and the Doctor called out to me. It surprised me that he should have known I was standing outside in the dark. I entered his room and he bid me sit on the piano bench next to him while he continued the fugue. . . . His powerful hands were in total control of the piano as he met Bach's demands for complete definition of each note—each with its own weight and value, yet all of them intimately laced together to create an ordered whole.
>
> . . . .
>
> He was now freed of the pressure and tensions of the

hospital, with its forms to fill out in triplicate and the mounting demands of officialdom; freed of the unanswered mail on his desk; freed of the heat and the saturating moisture and the fetishers and the ants that get into the medicines. . . . Now Bach was restoring him to a world of creative and ordered splendor.

(*Albert Schweitzer's Mission*)

Versatility is a hidden strength reservoir of the admired leader who comes to stay.

SHARING

The isolation of the frontier made sharing a necessity for common survival. It was the pioneer against the elements, the Indians, and the renegades. Neighbors were so few and distanced that the pioneers reached out for companionship. Family members were more important as friends than as blood brothers. The frontier gave focus to a guiding principle of my life: "It is not my role to see through people./It is my privilege to see people through."

Whether on the frontier of the old West or the new economic frontier of the Western world, the question is the ageless: "Am I my neighbor's keeper?" Leaders have a microphase approach to the world. They look at the world economically, culturally, religiously as a whole. To John Bryan, being born to the manor of privilege meant accepting some compensating sacrifice. It would never be the mere empty words of Shaw in *Major Barbara* about the rich in London helping the poor so the poor wouldn't complain about the rich. John would be on the cutting edge at the time the New South was seeking her soul.

Adam and Eve's struggle between ownership and stewardship is not finished today. No generation is allowed to be a total consumer. Endless consumption is slow suicide. Felix Rohatyn of Lazard Frères, who among other ventures brought RCA/NBC into GE, addressed our contemporary vulgarity:

I've never seen the kind of money spent that people are spending today. It is conspicuous consumption without conscience. I frequently see women flying to Paris for a fitting and flying back on the *Concorde.*

John preserves art to develop spiritual traditions and to give birth to fresh and spontaneous values for today. While some executives view the earth as a resource to possess, a leader sees the earth as a community of people. Hear again the Dean of St. Paul's Cathedral: "Any man who marries the spirit of his age is soon to become a widower."

How does such a philosophy play in the Loop of Chicago? Here are excerpts from an address John Bryan, Jr. gave the Independent Sector at their annual conference October 28, 1986.

. . . For well over twenty-five years I've been fortunate enough to have the opportunity to provide leadership for, or be personally involved in community affairs to a rather substantial degree. . . .

It is my thesis that one absolutely *must* contribute one's time and talent to community activities. . . .

Let me discuss what I think are the principal self-interest motivations which corporations, and their executives, legitimately follow in their relationships with the community.

Given our strong obligation to shareholders, it is indeed proper for us to require that our business benefit from community involvement.

There are probably two types of motives that relate to the enlightened self-interests of the corporation. One is employee-related and has to do with the need for a business to support the community from which it draws its work force. Every company still recognizes that making its community a healthier, safer, and more pleasant place to live pays real dividends. Everything from the quality of the school system, to the availability of recreational and cultural activities, contributes to securing and keeping good employees.

Second, there is no question that many companies have been motivated to become more socially responsible out of a concern for their image with the public. No company in our society—no matter how profitable—is considered excellent if it does not meet its obligations in the area of public responsibility. Conversely, a company that does operate within that tradition finds it easier to hire the best people and easier to sell products.

Competitive instincts are inherent in man. We keep score in everything, trying to be the best—competing. Are we creating enough peer pressure between companies with regard to their contributions in the area of social responsibility?

There's a *Fortune* 500—there's a *Forbes* 1,000. The businesses of America get ranked by every kind of conceivable measure, subjective and objective. Yet, somehow we seem bashful about ranking corporations and their managements in the area of public responsibility. By doing this, however, there is, in my judgment, a marvelous opportunity to cause managements in corporate America to focus more attention on public responsibility.

At the Sara Lee Corporation, we have issued specific directives which state our standards and expectations concerning (1) contributions, and (2) civic involvement.

The generally accepted level of giving for good corporate citizens is 2 percent of pre-tax profits. Not surprisingly, that is also our publicly stated policy. Now, as it happens, in recent years we have substantially exceeded that goal—in part, because of an extensive product donation program that contributes millions of dollars worth of goods each year—principally to food banks affiliated with the Second Harvest Network.

With respect to how we contribute, our giving is focused in three general areas.

The first is to organizations chosen by our employees. As you know, individuals provide approximately 90 percent of all private giving, and we encourage employee contributions through a matching grants program that is quite liberal. Contributions up to $1,000 per employee are matched by the company on a two-to-one basis. Additional donations are matched dollar for dollar—up to a maximum of $10,000 per employee per year.

Our second major emphasis in corporate giving is to arts and cultural organizations. We believe this area is important because preserving and encouraging a community's creative resources so clearly enriches the overall quality of life.

The largest share of our contributions is directed to programs that aid the disadvantaged. This includes programs in the areas of economic development and assistance, and reflects our special interest in projects that are directed to minorities. . . .

We also make our expectations clear to Sara Lee Corporation managers. The message is simple—community involvement is basic to being a responsible business executive. We reinforce this idea by having all executives list their outside activities as part of the manpower review process every year. Inside the company, we set specific goals for our managers with respect to areas like affirmative action, minority relations, and employee health and safety.

Blending Stewardship and Success

In food retailing, we revere the Rabb name from Boston. The late Sidney Rabb and brother Irving have matched every business step forward with a broader charitable concern. The Bible says: "Give, and it will be given to you: good measure, pressed down, shaken together, and running over will be put into your bosom. For with the same measure that you use, it will be measured back to you."

The Bible suggests that our capacity to receive is dependent upon making room by letting our generosity flow out. In my own city, I watched George Erath for thirty years. From professional athletics, he moved to woods and veneers; and every time I turn around, he and his wife Shirley are making a significant charitable gift or taking a leadership role on a voluntary board. George commented:

> I believe that the church teachings and family practices have the greatest bearing on one's attitude toward giving.

> Recognizing the fact that we are stewards for that which we possess during our time on earth is certainly the teaching of the church. Sharing the rewards of your talents with others is a teaching that came from my parents. In addition, I had the good fortune of having my first financial business partner believe that no one does anything alone and one must always remember those who helped along the way and plow back in these institutions a portion of the rewards that come as a business prospers.

The Pardees of Pacific Palisades—George, Hoyt and Doug—have become valued friends. George started their building business modestly in 1948. Hoyt and Doug joined as they finished college. When they merged with Weyerhauser in 1969, they had built thirty thousand homes and twenty five shopping centers. They pledged at the beginning that they would not make any decision unless all three were in agreement. What is the secret of such harmony? I don't know three men more consistently generous to a wide variety of causes with the greater emphasis on education and youth. Their mutual generosity was the glue that kept them on the same track. Little wonder their building peers had them inducted into their hall of fame.

Jack C. D. Bailey wouldn't puncture our balloons, but would remind us that charity begins at home. A generous person, Jack has built Franchise Enterprises into one hundred fast-food restaurants. At his annual managers' meeting he, without notice, announced he was giving shares of his privately held company to each of them. Not only did it give them instant worth but, if the company goes public as planned, their estates will be enhanced. Is there a better way to gain loyalty than by sharing?

▐▌

In this chapter we've used mainly John Bryan to let us see executive statesmanship. According to Norman Cousins (*Albert Schweitzer's Mission*) Dr. Albert Schweitzer wrote that

> The scholar . . . must not live for science alone, nor the businessman for his business, nor the artist for his art. If

affirmation for life is genuine, it will "demand from all that they should sacrifice a portion of their lives for others."

This insight from Dr. Norman Cousins effectively concludes this chapter for all of us who seek "staying power".

We live at a time when people seem afraid to be themselves, when they seem to prefer a hard, shiny exterior to the genuineness of deeply felt emotion. Sophistication is prized and sentiment is dreaded. It is made to appear that one of the worst blights on a reputation is to be called a do-gooder. The literature of the day is remarkably devoid of themes on the natural goodness . . . of man, seeing no dramatic power in the most powerful fact of the human mixture. The values of time lean to a phony toughness, casual violence, cheap emotion. . . .

The tragedy in life is not in the hurt to a man's name or even in the fact of death itself. The tragedy of life is in what dies inside a man while he lives—the death of genuine feeling, the death of inspired response, the death of awareness that makes it possible to feel the pain or the glory of other men in oneself. . . .

Much of the ache and the brooding unhappiness in modern man is the result of his difficulty in using himself fully. He performs compartmentalized tasks in a compartmentalized world. He is reined in—physically, socially, spiritually. Only rarely does he have a sense of fulfilling himself through total contact with a challenge. He finds it difficult to make real connections even with those who are near him. But there are vast urges of conscience, natural purpose, and goodness inside him demanding air and release. And he has his own potentialities, the regions of which are far broader than he can even guess at—potentialities that keep nagging at him to be fully used.

(*Albert Schweitzer's Mission*)

12

God Willing and the Creeks Don't Rise

In its celluloid documentation of the West, Hollywood's greatest oversight, either intentional or accidental, was the influence of religion, via Bible or preacher, on the western travelers. John Wayne's occasional reference to "pilgrims" is the only evidence we have that just maybe the power of the Eternal might have helped the Westerners in their time of need.

Nothing could be further from the truth. It was not just the Mormons or the Jesuit Missionaries who carried the Word of God out West. Buried in every family trunk was that well-worn copy of Holy Writ, complete with all the birthdays, marriages, and deaths that the family was heir to.

It was a source of prayer, a school book for the young, a diary of the trek, a power and a discipline by which one could live and survive in a wilderness bent upon one's destruction. It was consulted not only every Sunday, but many evenings by the fire and certainly at every marriage and death. To many it provided a latter-day guide to the land of plenty they sought.

There was no shame or embarrassment if one drew strength and consolation from the Word of God. Even the thieves and ruffians, grudgingly suspicious of its unseen power, were awed by those who used it.

Today, if the cavalry ain't comin', a deep sense of the Almighty still causes us to look inward to measure and gather our strength. It doesn't take much looking to realize we need something greater than ourselves, and fortunately, that something is a Someone who gives us our courage.

America Needs "Great Awakening II"

In my little notebook of prayer requests, after I have thought about all the different problems that I have wanted to discuss with God, I write in each day, "G.A. II," meaning, "O God, may we have 'Great Awakening II'?"

Out of "Great Awakening I," espoused and preached by George Whitefield in 1740, we received such beneficial by-products as our public education system, colleges and universities, workers' rights, greater dignity for women, and a renewed drive for freedom and tolerance in religious and philosophic matters.

George Whitefield, although born and educated in England, made seven trips to the New World, preaching over eight thousand times from the Carolinas to New England. Historians note that:

> His central emphasis was not the majesty but the Love of God; he proclaimed not divine wrath, judgment and retribution, but divine mercy and patience, divine pardon and grace . . . his ministry was tender, healing and inspiring. He loved the world . . . he had no preferences but in favor of the ignorant, the miserable and the poor.

Whitefield believed and preached that the wisdom, strength, and power of the Bible was not just for the highborn and educated, but also for the common people, if only they would take hold of it.

I like to believe that in some small measure the progress and courage that flowed from that first Awakening is starting to flow again. The common people are waking up. The rebirth of the Christian Spirit in all facets of American life is slowly, but very surely, beginning to be felt. This is a megatrend that John Naisbitt missed.

Prayer groups and Bible sessions are popping up in the most unlikely places: factories, board rooms, sports fields, even Wall Street. The awakening is not limited to churches, television ministries, or gospel FM stations. Executives as well as line-employees are finding places and times in their busy schedules to pay homage to the Almighty.

This reawakening should not strike us as odd. After all the United States Congress opens each daily session with an official invocation to God. Our coins and bills still carry the motto, In God We Trust. That statement is not a declaration that God is necessarily on our side, but that, as Abraham Lincoln said, "It is imperative that we be on God's side."

In its scrupulous avoidance of any taint of religion in our civil life, the U.S. Supreme Court has, over the last half-century, erected a high barrier between the religious needs and the civil rights of Americans. The high-water mark of the Court's denial of religious practice in the normal places most people congregate has been effectively reached.

The "Great Awakening II" will not be denied because it springs, not from any one sect, congregation, or church, but from the very deepest need of the human personality. And like a river unnaturally dammed, this need for God's help in our daily life, has formed a huge, deep lake in the consciousness of the American public. I see cracks in the dam. It is leaking. Tomorrow?

Professor W. E. Hocking argued many years ago that we cannot have a sound society unless we have a sufficient number of people who cannot be bought. He called these the "unpurchasable people." He felt that no society can last long unless it has a quorum of people whose integrity nothing can buy. We used to call these "men of principle." Today, we have become a nation of chameleons.

Perhaps we have infected ourselves. To sell our products, we have analyzed, dissected, and cordoned off our product-buying public into as many individuated groups as we can conceive: married women, working, nonworking, Yuppies, blacks, traditionalists, young-angries, me-generations, Vietnam veterans, computer-oriented, futurists. The lists go on and on. And each one of these groups, we feel, must be pleased and placated, or we will miss them in the marketplace. And so, chameleonlike, we change our products and our personalities to conform with the whimsies we perceive, until finally we don't know what color we really are. In fact, we don't know who we are. By standing for all, we stand for none. The last position we want is to "stand up and be counted" as persons or companies of principle. We have become purchasable.

The first time I ever questioned whether I was "purchasable" or not was in 1954 when I was still serving as a parish minister. Fortunately the emphasis had always been placed on how our church could serve the people, and I made it a rule never to discuss my personal income, which is probably the best way to have good income. Our church was relatively new, yet they were paying me $10,000, which was a large sum for a minister in 1954, plus some attractive perks. A representative of H. L. Hunt called on me and said that Mr. Hunt was interested in my serving as the spokesman of his nationwide radio program. The starting salary would be $60,000. Now I wish I could write and say it never entered my mind to accept it, but for a boy raised with my modest background, $60,000 in 1954 was more than I thought I would ever make as income.

As the interviewer kept talking, the decision became clear, for I began to wonder whether Mr. Hunt, though admired for the fortune he made in oil, was a great patriot who cared about the United States or really only concerned about protecting himself.

That is one of the fine lines among those of us who call ourselves conservatives. Do we want that which is best for America or that which is best for ourselves? They are often not the same. What has been called conservative politics is more lenient and indulgent when it comes to business. When I learned that Mr. Hunt would have the final word on the scripts, and would have to approve everything I said, I began to understand Hocking's "unpurchasable people."

In my own city is a fine attorney by the name of Perry Keziah. He could be living on easy street as a corporate attorney. But years ago at the very beginning of a takeover attempt of his firm, all he had to do as the attorney of record was cooperate, keep his mouth shut, and walk away wealthy. He wouldn't do it and instead chose to resist.

Perry has a good law practice in our city today, but not the luxurious income he could have had if he had not walked away from the offer he felt was deceptive and ruinous to the people who originally built the company. Perry paid the price, but he has gained the towering respect of his friends and peers.

The Difference Between Ethics and Morals

Many people do not understand the critical difference between ethical and moral principles. Ethical principles are derived from the common consent of the populace as to what is right, whereas moral principles flow from the sum of beliefs of a religious creed. Moral principles give life, meaning, and definition to ethical principles. In descending order, then, ethical principles rank above civil law and give life, meaning, and definition to law.

Wilhelm Roepke, the German economist, noted:

> The market, competition and the play of supply and demand do not create ethical reserves; they presuppose them and they consume them. These reserves have to come from outside the market and no textbook on economics can replace them.
>
> Self-discipline, a sense of justice, honesty, fairness, chivalry, moderation, public spirit, respect for human dignity and firm ethical norms . . . all of these are the things which people must possess before they can go to the market and compete with each other.

Unfortunately, today, the ethical principles by which most Americans live can be summed up by the pagan Roman admonition: "No sin discovered, no sin committed." No wonder the marketplace is chaotic with the proliferation of consumer laws to force us to a morality.

In recent years we have fallen into a trap that determines our convictions, both public and private, by a deteriorating ethical consensus. Our convictions should be determined from deeply held religious beliefs. For if a society derives its guidelines from its ethical consensus alone, it will stagnate and then deteriorate.

I totally reject the businessman who becomes "ethical"

because he feels his conduct otherwise "will not pay." His conversion to this ethical conduct is short-lived. As Upton Sinclair points out, "It is difficult to get a man to understand something when his salary depends upon his not understanding it."

But just as Joshua challenged the Israelites, "And if it seems evil to you to serve the LORD, choose for yourselves this day whom you will serve. . . . But as for me and my house, we will serve the LORD," we, too, must decide whom we shall serve. As President Reagan said, "A nation is measured not by justifying its gross national product or military power but the strength of its devotion to the principles and values that bind its people and define its character. . . . In recent years America's values almost seemed in exile." He was echoing two hundred years later statesman Daniel Webster who said; "The most important thought that ever entered my mind is my personal accountability to Almighty God."

Am I, even for a moment, implying that a CEO become "so heavenly-minded that he is no earthly good"? No. Neither am I condoning our being so earthly-minded that we lose any heavenly value. On May 4, 1986, the eighty-four-year-young William Golub was honored at the tenth FMI Supermarket Industry Convention at McCormick Place, Chicago. We respect Bill for building a life through faith, opportunity, and self-reliance. The Price Chopper Supermarkets headquartered in Schenectady, New York, and now led by his able son, Neil, are only a bit of the tangible evidence that this man is a premier who has moved from one frontier to another.

My wife, Buren, was privileged to be a seatmate with Bill from Dallas to Atlanta several years ago. At her request, he enunciated his personal convictions:

> One's life should be built on principles and integrity. It should be deeply rooted in the finest principles of American free enterprise.
>
> One's life should be built on self-reliance, courage, and faith in Almighty God. It should be based on the dedication to go His way, to "Do unto others as you would have others do unto you."

213

"No man is an island. . . ." For we gather strength and purpose from those with whom we associate and work. . . .

Truly, life is a golden legacy to behold and treasure! And I feel blessed among men with nearly fourscore years of living.

Underlying my life through all the years have been my prayers to continue the privilege of doing His work. Sincerely and without attempting to sound "holier than thou," my prayers have been for guidance—never for material or personal gain. And as a result, my continuing blessings have been manifold and sometimes staggering. . . .

Let's move from Bill Golub in the Northeast to Bill Turner in Columbus, Georgia.

Bill is chairman of the board of the W. C. Bradley Company, a family of diverse and dynamic corporations. His full name is William Bradley Turner, and he presides over the business his maternal grandfather started in 1895. In 1919 Mr. Bradley paid $25 million for the Coca-Cola rights in the United States and Cuba. Immediately he recruited young Bob Woodruff of White Motor Company to return to his native Georgia and develop the soft drink territory. The rest is history! Today Bill serves on the board of Coca-Cola as a visionary outside director.

By age thirty two Bill Turner had gained corporate recognition in his own right, with honor after honor heaped upon him. As he told me:

Already I had experienced enough success to know more of the same would not bring me fulfillment. I was always trying to compete with myself.

Though I came from an affluent home with a grandfather and father among Georgia's most revered, I had low self-esteem. Being accepted I felt depended on the way I performed. There wasn't any room for failure. I wasn't able to say, "Well, I blew that one; forgive me."

Our staid old company I had positioned for today. The demands for a foundry, heavy steel, railroad needs had diminished, but in their place were companies like

CharBroil, Bradley's Direct Marketing, Bradley Farm Division, Jordan and Bradley Building Supply, and N.S.S.I. Enterprises. Increasingly I took interest in Columbus Bank and Trust Company where we had a strong family position, and in 1982 I succeeded my dad as chairman.

After the Navy, I married the one lady I had wanted to be my wife since she was twelve. So now, with my business jelling and she busy birthing and raising our six children, I diligently gave my time to the Boy's Clubs, YMCA, the United Way, and other worthy charitable causes that cried for help. Yes, I was doing the right things for the wrong reasons. I wanted the recognition that I had witnessed others receiving for doing those things.

My minister asked me to teach a fifth grade church class. When I responded that I wasn't equipped intellectually and certainly not spiritually to do this, he said, "Bill, just be open and honest with the kids; and when you talk about Jesus Christ, just tell 'em what you personally know about Him." Well, I didn't have much to share about Jesus, so for a year I talked about Babe Ruth, Lou Gehrig, Joe DiMaggio, and Charley Trippi.

Still I was hungry for more in life than the superficial "highs" that another business deal or award gave me. Shortly after being honored by our local Chamber of Commerce, I went home and prayed in desperation for God to make me real. What others saw as peaks in my life I found to be the pits, and I needed Him to pull me out.

Just a few days after the prayer, a respected friend from Atlanta invited me to join him at the Layman's Leadership Institute in Miami, Florida. There I heard fellow executives report how God had changed their lives and how they felt a partnership with Him in their corporate decisions. They were devoid of any pious or holier-than-thou attitude. They were tough but possessing a strange warmth and magnetism. In those moments I told the Lord I wanted to let go and offer my life for His glory.

This changed my leadership motivation at the W. C. Bradley Company. It became evident in my home when I slowed my frenzied pace, stopped my eating on the run, and daily joined Sue Marie and our growing brood in family devotions.

For thirty years now we've built our business schedules, our national and international travel, around missing very few Sundays from our church where I now teach seventeen-year-olds.

In our company I want our employees to know management cares about them and we expect them to care about each other. I don't think the profit motive or job security is enough to make work ennobling. Without being paternal, we want to subtly create an atmosphere where our employees grow materially, intellectually, and spiritually. We let them know together we can build not only better products but a better world. From a portion of the profits we fund the Bradley Center, a psychiatric center. When an employee is having problems and wants help, we arrange for the employee to visit the Pastoral Institute to receive the benefit of trained counseling. The Bradley Center not only helps the employees of the corporation in our area but has special research and outreach programs for teenagers. The theme of the Center comes from Isaiah's prophecy to Israel, "Comfort, yes, comfort My people!"

Bill Turner's favorite verse also comes from Isaiah: "The people who walked in darkness/Have seen a great light." Being around him even for a moment makes me sense you are with an enlightened leader.

Bill Turner's approach to life might be summed up in the opening lines of a speech prepared for Laity Sunday, September 28, 1986: "God doesn't want people to know how good you are, He wants them to know how good they are."

The New Pilgrims of Progress

A 1982 study on America's values, commissioned by the Connecticut Mutual Life Insurance Company, discovered that the desire for religious commitment penetrated "virtually every dimension of American experience." Further, the survey indicated that at least 45 million Americans unashamedly called themselves intensely religious. I call that a crack in the humanistic dike.

The survey indicated that leadership in law, education, business, government, military, communications, and science, as well as the public at large, was seeking a renewed personal relationship with God, though not necessarily related to attendance at a local worship center. These are the "new pilgrims" in search of progress.

By contrast, only 14 percent of the American public, polled in 1984 by the Opinion Research Corporation, expressed a high level of trust and confidence in large corporations. These corporations were rated very poorly on ethics, morality, job creation, protection of the environment, and meeting social needs. Is somebody off base here? If we have a public that is growing increasingly aware of religious morals and American corporations that are perceived as increasingly amoral, somewhere, somehow, something has got to give. I am afraid it will be the American products that will lose respect in the marketplace since I believe quality and morality interlock.

The distinguished psychiatrist, Erik Erikson, teaches that maturity cannot be reached until there is fidelity to an ideal, a value, a belief. The challenge to American government, business, and education seems incontrovertible. We must find those principles that are so sacred that they can never, never be compromised. We must never excuse our indifferences under the blanket of tolerance.

Principles are like a two-edged sword. When you bend them, the edges cut.

To staunch the flow, it is time we stop trying to bend principle to get our market share. It is time to live up to what we say we believe.

These are challenges for mature people. These are challenges that the marketplace is demanding that we answer. These are challenges that the Almighty would have us remember as Israel of old:

> For the LORD your God is bringing you into a good land, a land of brooks of water, of fountains and springs, that flow out of valleys and hills. . . .
>
> When you have eaten and are full, then you shall bless the LORD your God for the good land which He has given you.
>
> Beware that you do not forget the LORD your God by

not keeping His commandments, His judgments, and His statutes which I command you today, lest—when you have eaten and are full, and have built beautiful houses and dwell in them . . . and you forget the LORD your God who brought you out of the land of Egypt, from the house of bondage . . . then you say in your heart, "My power and the might of my hand have gained me this wealth."

And you shall remember the LORD your God, for it is He who gives you power to get wealth, that He may establish His covenant which He swore to your fathers, as it is this day.

(Deuteronomy 8)

So after many pages we stand together on our frontier of the twenty-first century. As on every frontier, there are tangibles and intangibles. We are not just scorched by the prairie breezes, but in the distance ominous black funnels twist.

With our workplace and homeplace equally threatened, the cry goes out for leaders: those unpurchasable leaders who will rise above the dangers of avarice, careerism, status-seeking, money, power, and reputation; those who are willing to live on the frontier looking back through past experiences for confidence as they face forward with resolution.

Afterword

In the Foreword, I mentioned one of the most dominant influences of my life, Mildred Steere Haggai, who inspired me to face courageously any and all challenges that came my way, not to flinch when called upon to serve as a leader. Let me tell you now of the other dominant influence in my life, my father, Waddy Abraham Haggai.

On July 4, 1986, Buren and I traveled to the Statue of Liberty ceremonies in New York City. We were aboard one of those forty thousand ships in the harbor that ran the gamut from the majestic *QE II* and our president's aircraft carrier to a little rowboat with two fellows and an American flag propped up between them. Actually, we had the best of all worlds. We were caught up in the excitement of being there in person, and then on each corner of the decks, we could see all the ceremonies on television.

In the midst of all that excitement, Buren noticed that I really "wasn't with them" and asked where I was in my thinking. My response was that I was not at any other place but I certainly was in another year. In fact I was all the way back to the year 1912, and I was thinking about one of those nameless ships that slowly, laboriously plowed the waves of the North Atlantic. Seasickness was the rule rather than the exception, but the decks were kept clean by the sweep of the waves as the ship dipped and groaned as it rose again. Jammed on board were people from a variety of countries on Mediterranean shores. It had been a placid voyage in the first days but at Gibraltar, calm waters and resting seas would become only a memory. In the midst of the crowd was a little fellow about 5'6" with bushy black hair and eyebrows. He carried comfortably on his face the heritage from a father born at the foot of Mt. Herman and a mother born in Beirut.

Educated well in the Greek Orthodox schools of his land, he could speak French, Russian, and Arabic—and, yes, even four words of English, "Yes, Jesus loves me." His voyage was not a holiday or vacation but an escape, for religious persecution is not a new hazard of that part of the world. He was fleeing the cruel heel of the newest Turkish Sultan who, to prove his machismo, would sweep down upon the little country of Syria (and Lebanon was a part of Syria at that time) and bloody up some Christians as preventive medicine against any rebellion.

The voyage seemed endless until finally came the cry, "There is land—there is land!" Rising out of the ocean was the silhouette of New York City. As the ship drew nearer, it seemed only proper that the first person to greet the passengers would be an immigrant who, too, had found the freedom that a democratic republic called the United States of America had to offer. The immigrant was a beautiful lady. Dressed in restful green, she stood tall upon her perch, a torch in her hand so she could see clearly into the faces of the people so crowding the deck that the ship seemed to list to its side. Standing where the Hudson was flowing into the Atlantic, she looked down upon that ship and said in perfect Yiddish, "If you're looking for a land that has 'In God we Trust' as an explanation more than a motto—welcome."

In perfect Italian she said, "If your heart is warm, made for loving and not for warring—welcome to a land that you may love and that will love you back in return."

In perfect Greek she said, "If you're in despair that your city-states are a free government gone sour, I give you cities and states who glory not in their past but eagerly await their future."

In perfect Arabic she said, "If you've been beaten because of your faith in God through Christ and have been afraid of the night lest it would mean no more sun, I welcome you to a land of mornings where the sun comes up as a proper reflection of God's eternal promises."

Then she paused and again in perfect Yiddish, Italian, Greek, and Arabic said, "This land will not give you anything, but it will allow you, by the grace of God, to be what you choose to be."

The little lad, too short to see and surrounded by the taller people around him, heard her promise in Arabic, and he believed her. So, like millions of Americans, my father came to the United States.

Now in 1986 I was looking at the lady. She was one-hundred years old but had become more beautiful with the passing of years, as women so often do. Green was still becoming to her, but it was new. Undimmed by age, her eyes had a renewed sparkle, and so she could see every person passing her more clearly. She even asked the President of the United States to give her a new torch with a brighter light.

I call that lad I was thinking about Daddy; he is eighty-nine now and has been blessed with remarkable health. If you were to go to his modest condominium in Decatur, Georgia, and say, "Waddy, is America as great as you had dreamed or thought?" He would quickly tell you, "No, the United States is much greater than I ever could have dreamed or thought."

Dad's frontier was easier to define than ours, but Dad has believed he could make a difference. Shy, retiring, somewhat insecure, small of stature, he felt it was not necessary for him to decide whether or not he was a leader. His job was to accomplish the tasks set before him and let others judge him and the results. He felt the blessings he had received demanded no less. We have been the recipients of unparalleled liberty, cultural advantage, and wealth. That is where we come from. Time has verified the experiment. The future has no guarantee. The creek may rise. We can fail, but we will only be failures if we refuse to take the mantle of leadership with spirit, courage, and intelligence.

That is the only chance for the best to win in the twenty-first century.

Acknowledgments

Richard L. Federer
Vice President
Communications Group
Wetterau, Incorporated

Dick Federer wrote with me sentence by sentence in the search for *How the Best Is Won*. Intellectual, keen, and versatile, Dick, an acquaintance of years, first took time to understand me and then apply his resourcefulness in helping me write what I wanted to say. An accomplished writer himself, he willingly locked himself into my mindset. Contrary to popular assumption, writing is a foreign discipline to a speaker. All of my life I've been preparing speeches with phrases, dots, dashes. Dick had to take the pieces and fragments and mold them together.

Dick N. Dalton
Senior Vice President
Communications and Strategic Planning
Wetterau, Incorporated

When I became disheartened and tentative, Dick Dalton kept telling me, "There's a book in you. Now let the reader see the people you identify but let them be seen as you view them so the readers understand how you value leadership. You keep the book focused in your heart and we'll pull it out."

Sam Moore
CEO
Thomas Nelson, Inc.

Since 1953 we have been friends. He personifies the premises of this book. Arriving at my doorstep in Rock Hill, South

Carolina, he had the worst case of "broken English" I had heard. It was easier to read his facial expressions than to understand his words. At the time, he was selling books door-to-door while simultaneously completing degrees with honors at Columbia Bible College and the University of South Carolina. When in later years he acquired the stately old Thomas Nelson Company, he asked that I do a book on leadership emphasizing the quality of the leader more than the style. I was determined to gain a half century of experience before doing so. But, when and if I did write, there was never any question who would be the publisher.

John E. Haggai
Chairman
Haggai Institute

Whatever an older brother should be, he is. He has believed in my abilities more than I have. He encouraged my taking to the pulpit at age twelve. He has accepted me at my worst and pushed me to be my best. A skillful writer himself (*How To Win Over Worry; My Son Johnny; Lead On*), he had had a singular message for me in recent years: "Write, write, write." A bonus since 1945 has been his talented wife, Christine, my first sister.

The late Ted Haggai
Senior Scientist
Hughes Corporation

He was the "good humor man" in my life. He kept me loose. Although we often disagreed I doubt that we had a dozen unpleasant words. While I admired his flights to the unknown, armed only with equations, he was fascinated by my patience with people, who are never fully known. He never encouraged me as much as just believed there wasn't anything his "kid brother" couldn't do.

Mary Helen Batten
Secretary-Treasurer
Tom Haggai and Associates, Inc.

For almost twenty years, Mary Helen has been my trusted associate and friend. She has managed my office, my travel schedule, the booking of appearances, and personal finances. During the four years this book has been forming in my mind and on paper, Mary Helen has translated my handwriting into typewritten page after page, rewrite after rewrite. Without her patience and general knowledge of the way I think, this book would never have reached the editors.

These, too, I must acknowledge in the area noted:
Emory Bogardus, sociology
Phillips Brooks, ministry
Robert J. Brown, racial understanding
Winston Churchill, statesmanship
Charles T. Clayton, salemanship
Robert E. Coleman, pragmatism
Norman Coursins, literature
Peter Drucker, management
Gerow Hodges, service
William James, philosophy
Morris Lewis, Jr., entrepreneurship
Albert Schweitzer, humanities
Charles Haddon Spurgeon, homiletics
Robert Taft, politics
Arnold Toynbee, history

Index

3M, 116
Abraham, 21, 24-25, 44
Adams, Harry, 53
Aders, Robert O., 61
Albertson's, 84
Alexander, W. W., 35
Allegheny Corporation, 73
Allied Expert Systems, Inc., 55
Allsopp, Tom, 167-168
Allumbaugh, Byron, 63
American Cast Iron Pipe, 35
American Psychological Association, 180
American Stock Exchange, 69
Amiel, Henri Frederic, 85
Amon, Tony, 131
Argonne National Laboratory, 41
Atwater, Jr., Bruce, 99
Ayoub, Sam, 131

Bach, 201-2
Bailey, Jack C. D., 206
Batten, Mary Helen, 125-126
Belk-Lindsey, 142
Belk, John M., 141-143
Belk, William Henry, 141
Ben Franklin store, 190
Bere, James F., 159
Berle, Adolph, 94
Berry, John, 151
Berry, Loren M., 150-154
Bliss, Edwin, 123
Boetcker, William, 125
Bok, Edward, 175
Borg-Warner, 159
Borman, Colonel Frank, 138, 149, 166
Boy Scouts of America 23, 73, 81, 167
Boy's Clubs, 142, 215
Boyson, Rhodes, 62
Bozzuto, 127
Bradley Center, 216
Briston Bar and Grille, 164, 165
Brockton Enterprise, The, 98
Bronowski, Jacob, 197
Brooks, Phillips, 29
Brown, Pat, 189
Browning, Robert, 75
Bryan, John, H., 63, 197-200, 202, 203, 206
Buddha, 155
Bunyan, John, 155
Burke, Jim, 81
Burke, Edmund, 174
Burlington Industries, 94
Burroughs, John, 175, 201

Burroughs, P. E., 155
Buxton, Charles, 179
Byron, Fletcher, 168

CBS, 84, 101, 161-163
Caleb, 96
Caldwell, Harriett, 189
California Retailers Association, 64
Campbell Soup Company, 22
Campbell, Jack, 123-125
Cannon, Charles, 102
Carnegie, Andrew, 197
Carolina Underwear, 76
Carr, E. H., 18
Carr, Guy, 28
Carter, Jimmy, 122, 155
Chesterton, G. K., 77
Cincinnati Royals, 177
Clarke, Sir Kenneth, 40
Club Aluminum, 78
Coca-Cola, 21, 130-131, 133, 137-138, 140, 214
Coleridge, Samuel Taylor, 174
Columbus Bank and Trust Company, 215
Conference Board, 55
Connecticut Mutual Life Insurance Company, 216
Consolidated Company, 198
Continental Illinois Bank, 182
Convergent Technologies, 133
Coolidge, Calvin, 30, 116
Corbett, Bruce, 97, 100
Cosby, Philip B., 94, 99
Cotting, Jim, 35
Cousins, Norman, 100, 189, 201, 206-207
Covington, J. Harris, 179-181
Crick, F. H. C., 91
Criswell, W. A., 187
Croce, Benedetto, 84
Crocker, Jack, 62
Crook, George, 37
Crowell, Grace, 188
Cuccaro, Ernie, 123
Cummings, Nathan, 199
Cummins Engines, 17
Cunningham, Bob, 131
Currie, Sir Arthur, 199
Custer, General George, 171

Dalton, Richard, 185
Dartnell, 152
David, 60
David, John, 122

225